C-3449   CAREER EXAMINATION SERIES

This is your
PASSBOOK for...

General Maintainer

Test Preparation Study Guide
Questions & Answers

COPYRIGHT NOTICE

This book is SOLELY intended for, is sold ONLY to, and its use is RESTRICTED to individual, bona fide applicants or candidates who qualify by virtue of having seriously filed applications for appropriate license, certificate, professional and/or promotional advancement, higher school matriculation, scholarship, or other legitimate requirements of education and/or governmental authorities.

This book is NOT intended for use, class instruction, tutoring, training, duplication, copying, reprinting, excerption, or adaptation, etc., by:

1) Other publishers
2) Proprietors and/or Instructors of "Coaching" and/or Preparatory Courses
3) Personnel and/or Training Divisions of commercial, industrial, and governmental organizations
4) Schools, colleges, or universities and/or their departments and staffs, including teachers and other personnel
5) Testing Agencies or Bureaus
6) Study groups which seek by the purchase of a single volume to copy and/or duplicate and/or adapt this material for use by the group as a whole without having purchased individual volumes for each of the members of the group
7) Et al.

Such persons would be in violation of appropriate Federal and State statutes.

PROVISION OF LICENSING AGREEMENTS – Recognized educational, commercial, industrial, and governmental institutions and organizations, and others legitimately engaged in educational pursuits, including training, testing, and measurement activities, may address request for a licensing agreement to the copyright owners, who will determine whether, and under what conditions, including fees and charges, the materials in this book may be used them. In other words, a licensing facility exists for the legitimate use of the material in this book on other than an individual basis. However, it is asseverated and affirmed here that the material in this book CANNOT be used without the receipt of the express permission of such a licensing agreement from the Publishers. Inquiries re licensing should be addressed to the company, attention rights and permissions department.

All rights reserved, including the right of reproduction in whole or in part, in any form or by any means, electronic or mechanical, including photocopying, recording, or by any information storage and retrieval system, without permission in writing from the Publisher.

Copyright © 2024 by
National Learning Corporation

212 Michael Drive, Syosset, NY 11791
(516) 921-8888 • www.passbooks.com
E-mail: info@passbooks.com

PASSBOOK® SERIES

THE *PASSBOOK® SERIES* has been created to prepare applicants and candidates for the ultimate academic battlefield – the examination room.

At some time in our lives, each and every one of us may be required to take an examination – for validation, matriculation, admission, qualification, registration, certification, or licensure.

Based on the assumption that every applicant or candidate has met the basic formal educational standards, has taken the required number of courses, and read the necessary texts, the *PASSBOOK® SERIES* furnishes the one special preparation which may assure passing with confidence, instead of failing with insecurity. Examination questions – together with answers – are furnished as the basic vehicle for study so that the mysteries of the examination and its compounding difficulties may be eliminated or diminished by a sure method.

This book is meant to help you pass your examination provided that you qualify and are serious in your objective.

The entire field is reviewed through the huge store of content information which is succinctly presented through a provocative and challenging approach – the question-and-answer method.

A climate of success is established by furnishing the correct answers at the end of each test.

You soon learn to recognize types of questions, forms of questions, and patterns of questioning. You may even begin to anticipate expected outcomes.

You perceive that many questions are repeated or adapted so that you can gain acute insights, which may enable you to score many sure points.

You learn how to confront new questions, or types of questions, and to attack them confidently and work out the correct answers.

You note objectives and emphases, and recognize pitfalls and dangers, so that you may make positive educational adjustments.

Moreover, you are kept fully informed in relation to new concepts, methods, practices, and directions in the field.

You discover that you are actually taking the examination all the time: you are preparing for the examination by "taking" an examination, not by reading extraneous and/or supererogatory textbooks.

In short, this PASSBOOK®, used directedly, should be an important factor in helping you to pass your test.

GENERAL MAINTAINER

DUTIES
Under the general supervision of a Maintenance Supervisor or a journey-level mechanic, General Maintainers perform a variety of manual and semi-skilled work in accordance with established practices, work orders or instructions. Work typically requires the use of general maintenance skills and knowledge of a variety of trade fields such as carpentry, landscaping, painting, paving, roofing, structural and mechanical maintenance, and includes a working knowledge of materials, tools, and equipment of these trades.

SCOPE OF THE EXAMINATION
The <u>written test</u> will cover knowledge, skills and/or abilities in the above areas.

HOW TO TAKE A TEST

I. YOU MUST PASS AN EXAMINATION

A. *WHAT EVERY CANDIDATE SHOULD KNOW*

Examination applicants often ask us for help in preparing for the written test. What can I study in advance? What kinds of questions will be asked? How will the test be given? How will the papers be graded?

As an applicant for a civil service examination, you may be wondering about some of these things. Our purpose here is to suggest effective methods of advance study and to describe civil service examinations.

Your chances for success on this examination can be increased if you know how to prepare. Those "pre-examination jitters" can be reduced if you know what to expect. You can even experience an adventure in good citizenship if you know why civil service exams are given.

B. *WHY ARE CIVIL SERVICE EXAMINATIONS GIVEN?*

Civil service examinations are important to you in two ways. As a citizen, you want public jobs filled by employees who know how to do their work. As a job seeker, you want a fair chance to compete for that job on an equal footing with other candidates. The best-known means of accomplishing this two-fold goal is the competitive examination.

Exams are widely publicized throughout the nation. They may be administered for jobs in federal, state, city, municipal, town or village governments or agencies.

Any citizen may apply, with some limitations, such as the age or residence of applicants. Your experience and education may be reviewed to see whether you meet the requirements for the particular examination. When these requirements exist, they are reasonable and applied consistently to all applicants. Thus, a competitive examination may cause you some uneasiness now, but it is your privilege and safeguard.

C. *HOW ARE CIVIL SERVICE EXAMS DEVELOPED?*

Examinations are carefully written by trained technicians who are specialists in the field known as "psychological measurement," in consultation with recognized authorities in the field of work that the test will cover. These experts recommend the subject matter areas or skills to be tested; only those knowledges or skills important to your success on the job are included. The most reliable books and source materials available are used as references. Together, the experts and technicians judge the difficulty level of the questions.

Test technicians know how to phrase questions so that the problem is clearly stated. Their ethics do not permit "trick" or "catch" questions. Questions may have been tried out on sample groups, or subjected to statistical analysis, to determine their usefulness.

Written tests are often used in combination with performance tests, ratings of training and experience, and oral interviews. All of these measures combine to form the best-known means of finding the right person for the right job.

II. HOW TO PASS THE WRITTEN TEST

A. NATURE OF THE EXAMINATION

To prepare intelligently for civil service examinations, you should know how they differ from school examinations you have taken. In school you were assigned certain definite pages to read or subjects to cover. The examination questions were quite detailed and usually emphasized memory. Civil service exams, on the other hand, try to discover your present ability to perform the duties of a position, plus your potentiality to learn these duties. In other words, a civil service exam attempts to predict how successful you will be. Questions cover such a broad area that they cannot be as minute and detailed as school exam questions.

In the public service similar kinds of work, or positions, are grouped together in one "class." This process is known as *position-classification*. All the positions in a class are paid according to the salary range for that class. One class title covers all of these positions, and they are all tested by the same examination.

B. FOUR BASIC STEPS

1) Study the announcement

How, then, can you know what subjects to study? Our best answer is: "Learn as much as possible about the class of positions for which you've applied." The exam will test the knowledge, skills and abilities needed to do the work.

Your most valuable source of information about the position you want is the official exam announcement. This announcement lists the training and experience qualifications. Check these standards and apply only if you come reasonably close to meeting them.

The brief description of the position in the examination announcement offers some clues to the subjects which will be tested. Think about the job itself. Review the duties in your mind. Can you perform them, or are there some in which you are rusty? Fill in the blank spots in your preparation.

Many jurisdictions preview the written test in the exam announcement by including a section called "Knowledge and Abilities Required," "Scope of the Examination," or some similar heading. Here you will find out specifically what fields will be tested.

2) Review your own background

Once you learn in general what the position is all about, and what you need to know to do the work, ask yourself which subjects you already know fairly well and which need improvement. You may wonder whether to concentrate on improving your strong areas or on building some background in your fields of weakness. When the announcement has specified "some knowledge" or "considerable knowledge," or has used adjectives like "beginning principles of…" or "advanced … methods," you can get a clue as to the number and difficulty of questions to be asked in any given field. More questions, and hence broader coverage, would be included for those subjects which are more important in the work. Now weigh your strengths and weaknesses against the job requirements and prepare accordingly.

3) Determine the level of the position

Another way to tell how intensively you should prepare is to understand the level of the job for which you are applying. Is it the entering level? In other words, is this the position in which beginners in a field of work are hired? Or is it an intermediate or advanced level? Sometimes this is indicated by such words as "Junior" or "Senior" in the class title. Other jurisdictions use Roman numerals to designate the level – Clerk I, Clerk II, for example. The word "Supervisor" sometimes appears in the title. If the level is not indicated by the title, check the description of duties. Will you be working under very close supervision, or will you have responsibility for independent decisions in this work?

4) Choose appropriate study materials

Now that you know the subjects to be examined and the relative amount of each subject to be covered, you can choose suitable study materials. For beginning level jobs, or even advanced ones, if you have a pronounced weakness in some aspect of your training, read a modern, standard textbook in that field. Be sure it is up to date and has general coverage. Such books are normally available at your library, and the librarian will be glad to help you locate one. For entry-level positions, questions of appropriate difficulty are chosen – neither highly advanced questions, nor those too simple. Such questions require careful thought but not advanced training.

If the position for which you are applying is technical or advanced, you will read more advanced, specialized material. If you are already familiar with the basic principles of your field, elementary textbooks would waste your time. Concentrate on advanced textbooks and technical periodicals. Think through the concepts and review difficult problems in your field.

These are all general sources. You can get more ideas on your own initiative, following these leads. For example, training manuals and publications of the government agency which employs workers in your field can be useful, particularly for technical and professional positions. A letter or visit to the government department involved may result in more specific study suggestions, and certainly will provide you with a more definite idea of the exact nature of the position you are seeking.

III. KINDS OF TESTS

Tests are used for purposes other than measuring knowledge and ability to perform specified duties. For some positions, it is equally important to test ability to make adjustments to new situations or to profit from training. In others, basic mental abilities not dependent on information are essential. Questions which test these things may not appear as pertinent to the duties of the position as those which test for knowledge and information. Yet they are often highly important parts of a fair examination. For very general questions, it is almost impossible to help you direct your study efforts. What we can do is point out some of the more common of these general abilities needed in public service positions and describe some typical questions.

1) General information

Broad, general information has been found useful for predicting job success in some kinds of work. This is tested in a variety of ways, from vocabulary lists to questions about current events. Basic background in some field of work, such as sociology or economics, may be sampled in a group of questions. Often these are principles which have become familiar to most persons through exposure rather than through formal training. It is difficult to advise you how to study for these questions; being alert to the world around you is our best suggestion.

2) Verbal ability

An example of an ability needed in many positions is verbal or language ability. Verbal ability is, in brief, the ability to use and understand words. Vocabulary and grammar tests are typical measures of this ability. Reading comprehension or paragraph interpretation questions are common in many kinds of civil service tests. You are given a paragraph of written material and asked to find its central meaning.

3) Numerical ability

Number skills can be tested by the familiar arithmetic problem, by checking paired lists of numbers to see which are alike and which are different, or by interpreting charts and graphs. In the latter test, a graph may be printed in the test booklet which you are asked to use as the basis for answering questions.

4) Observation

A popular test for law-enforcement positions is the observation test. A picture is shown to you for several minutes, then taken away. Questions about the picture test your ability to observe both details and larger elements.

5) Following directions

In many positions in the public service, the employee must be able to carry out written instructions dependably and accurately. You may be given a chart with several columns, each column listing a variety of information. The questions require you to carry out directions involving the information given in the chart.

6) Skills and aptitudes

Performance tests effectively measure some manual skills and aptitudes. When the skill is one in which you are trained, such as typing or shorthand, you can practice. These tests are often very much like those given in business school or high school courses. For many of the other skills and aptitudes, however, no short-time preparation can be made. Skills and abilities natural to you or that you have developed throughout your lifetime are being tested.

Many of the general questions just described provide all the data needed to answer the questions and ask you to use your reasoning ability to find the answers. Your best preparation for these tests, as well as for tests of facts and ideas, is to be at your physical and mental best. You, no doubt, have your own methods of getting into an exam-taking mood and keeping "in shape." The next section lists some ideas on this subject.

IV. KINDS OF QUESTIONS

Only rarely is the "essay" question, which you answer in narrative form, used in civil service tests. Civil service tests are usually of the short-answer type. Full instructions for answering these questions will be given to you at the examination. But in case this is your first experience with short-answer questions and separate answer sheets, here is what you need to know:

1) Multiple-choice Questions

Most popular of the short-answer questions is the "multiple choice" or "best answer" question. It can be used, for example, to test for factual knowledge, ability to solve problems or judgment in meeting situations found at work.

A multiple-choice question is normally one of three types—
- It can begin with an incomplete statement followed by several possible endings. You are to find the one ending which *best* completes the statement, although some of the others may not be entirely wrong.
- It can also be a complete statement in the form of a question which is answered by choosing one of the statements listed.

- It can be in the form of a problem – again you select the best answer.

Here is an example of a multiple-choice question with a discussion which should give you some clues as to the method for choosing the right answer:

When an employee has a complaint about his assignment, the action which will *best* help him overcome his difficulty is to
   A. discuss his difficulty with his coworkers
   B. take the problem to the head of the organization
   C. take the problem to the person who gave him the assignment
   D. say nothing to anyone about his complaint

In answering this question, you should study each of the choices to find which is best. Consider choice "A" – Certainly an employee may discuss his complaint with fellow employees, but no change or improvement can result, and the complaint remains unresolved. Choice "B" is a poor choice since the head of the organization probably does not know what assignment you have been given, and taking your problem to him is known as "going over the head" of the supervisor. The supervisor, or person who made the assignment, is the person who can clarify it or correct any injustice. Choice "C" is, therefore, correct. To say nothing, as in choice "D," is unwise. Supervisors have and interest in knowing the problems employees are facing, and the employee is seeking a solution to his problem.

2) True/False Questions

The "true/false" or "right/wrong" form of question is sometimes used. Here a complete statement is given. Your job is to decide whether the statement is right or wrong.

SAMPLE: A roaming cell-phone call to a nearby city costs less than a non-roaming call to a distant city.

This statement is wrong, or false, since roaming calls are more expensive.
This is not a complete list of all possible question forms, although most of the others are variations of these common types. You will always get complete directions for answering questions. Be sure you understand *how* to mark your answers – ask questions until you do.

V. RECORDING YOUR ANSWERS

Computer terminals are used more and more today for many different kinds of exams.
For an examination with very few applicants, you may be told to record your answers in the test booklet itself. Separate answer sheets are much more common. If this separate answer sheet is to be scored by machine – and this is often the case – it is highly important that you mark your answers correctly in order to get credit.
An electronic scoring machine is often used in civil service offices because of the speed with which papers can be scored. Machine-scored answer sheets must be marked with a pencil, which will be given to you. This pencil has a high graphite content which responds to the electronic scoring machine. As a matter of fact, stray dots may register as answers, so do not let your pencil rest on the answer sheet while you are pondering the correct answer. Also, if your pencil lead breaks or is otherwise defective, ask for another.

Since the answer sheet will be dropped in a slot in the scoring machine, be careful not to bend the corners or get the paper crumpled.

The answer sheet normally has five vertical columns of numbers, with 30 numbers to a column. These numbers correspond to the question numbers in your test booklet. After each number, going across the page are four or five pairs of dotted lines. These short dotted lines have small letters or numbers above them. The first two pairs may also have a "T" or "F" above the letters. This indicates that the first two pairs only are to be used if the questions are of the true-false type. If the questions are multiple choice, disregard the "T" and "F" and pay attention only to the small letters or numbers.

Answer your questions in the manner of the sample that follows:

32. The largest city in the United States is
    A. Washington, D.C.
    B. New York City
    C. Chicago
    D. Detroit
    E. San Francisco

1) Choose the answer you think is best. (New York City is the largest, so "B" is correct.)
2) Find the row of dotted lines numbered the same as the question you are answering. (Find row number 32)
3) Find the pair of dotted lines corresponding to the answer. (Find the pair of lines under the mark "B.")
4) Make a solid black mark between the dotted lines.

VI. BEFORE THE TEST

Common sense will help you find procedures to follow to get ready for an examination. Too many of us, however, overlook these sensible measures. Indeed, nervousness and fatigue have been found to be the most serious reasons why applicants fail to do their best on civil service tests. Here is a list of reminders:

- Begin your preparation early – Don't wait until the last minute to go scurrying around for books and materials or to find out what the position is all about.
- Prepare continuously – An hour a night for a week is better than an all-night cram session. This has been definitely established. What is more, a night a week for a month will return better dividends than crowding your study into a shorter period of time.
- Locate the place of the exam – You have been sent a notice telling you when and where to report for the examination. If the location is in a different town or otherwise unfamiliar to you, it would be well to inquire the best route and learn something about the building.
- Relax the night before the test – Allow your mind to rest. Do not study at all that night. Plan some mild recreation or diversion; then go to bed early and get a good night's sleep.
- Get up early enough to make a leisurely trip to the place for the test – This way unforeseen events, traffic snarls, unfamiliar buildings, etc. will not upset you.
- Dress comfortably – A written test is not a fashion show. You will be known by number and not by name, so wear something comfortable.

- Leave excess paraphernalia at home – Shopping bags and odd bundles will get in your way. You need bring only the items mentioned in the official notice you received; usually everything you need is provided. Do not bring reference books to the exam. They will only confuse those last minutes and be taken away from you when in the test room.
- Arrive somewhat ahead of time – If because of transportation schedules you must get there very early, bring a newspaper or magazine to take your mind off yourself while waiting.
- Locate the examination room – When you have found the proper room, you will be directed to the seat or part of the room where you will sit. Sometimes you are given a sheet of instructions to read while you are waiting. Do not fill out any forms until you are told to do so; just read them and be prepared.
- Relax and prepare to listen to the instructions
- If you have any physical problem that may keep you from doing your best, be sure to tell the test administrator. If you are sick or in poor health, you really cannot do your best on the exam. You can come back and take the test some other time.

VII. AT THE TEST

The day of the test is here and you have the test booklet in your hand. The temptation to get going is very strong. Caution! There is more to success than knowing the right answers. You must know how to identify your papers and understand variations in the type of short-answer question used in this particular examination. Follow these suggestions for maximum results from your efforts:

1) Cooperate with the monitor

The test administrator has a duty to create a situation in which you can be as much at ease as possible. He will give instructions, tell you when to begin, check to see that you are marking your answer sheet correctly, and so on. He is not there to guard you, although he will see that your competitors do not take unfair advantage. He wants to help you do your best.

2) Listen to all instructions

Don't jump the gun! Wait until you understand all directions. In most civil service tests you get more time than you need to answer the questions. So don't be in a hurry. Read each word of instructions until you clearly understand the meaning. Study the examples, listen to all announcements and follow directions. Ask questions if you do not understand what to do.

3) Identify your papers

Civil service exams are usually identified by number only. You will be assigned a number; you must not put your name on your test papers. Be sure to copy your number correctly. Since more than one exam may be given, copy your exact examination title.

4) Plan your time

Unless you are told that a test is a "speed" or "rate of work" test, speed itself is usually not important. Time enough to answer all the questions will be provided, but this does not mean that you have all day. An overall time limit has been set. Divide the total time (in minutes) by the number of questions to determine the approximate time you have for each question.

5) Do not linger over difficult questions

If you come across a difficult question, mark it with a paper clip (useful to have along) and come back to it when you have been through the booklet. One caution if you do this – be sure to skip a number on your answer sheet as well. Check often to be sure that you have not lost your place and that you are marking in the row numbered the same as the question you are answering.

6) Read the questions

Be sure you know what the question asks! Many capable people are unsuccessful because they failed to *read* the questions correctly.

7) Answer all questions

Unless you have been instructed that a penalty will be deducted for incorrect answers, it is better to guess than to omit a question.

8) Speed tests

It is often better NOT to guess on speed tests. It has been found that on timed tests people are tempted to spend the last few seconds before time is called in marking answers at random – without even reading them – in the hope of picking up a few extra points. To discourage this practice, the instructions may warn you that your score will be "corrected" for guessing. That is, a penalty will be applied. The incorrect answers will be deducted from the correct ones, or some other penalty formula will be used.

9) Review your answers

If you finish before time is called, go back to the questions you guessed or omitted to give them further thought. Review other answers if you have time.

10) Return your test materials

If you are ready to leave before others have finished or time is called, take ALL your materials to the monitor and leave quietly. Never take any test material with you. The monitor can discover whose papers are not complete, and taking a test booklet may be grounds for disqualification.

VIII. EXAMINATION TECHNIQUES

1) Read the general instructions carefully. These are usually printed on the first page of the exam booklet. As a rule, these instructions refer to the timing of the examination; the fact that you should not start work until the signal and must stop work at a signal, etc. If there are any *special* instructions, such as a choice of questions to be answered, make sure that you note this instruction carefully.

2) When you are ready to start work on the examination, that is as soon as the signal has been given, read the instructions to each question booklet, underline any key words or phrases, such as *least, best, outline, describe* and the like. In this way you will tend to answer as requested rather than discover on reviewing your paper that you *listed without describing*, that you selected the *worst* choice rather than the *best* choice, etc.

3) If the examination is of the objective or multiple-choice type – that is, each question will also give a series of possible answers: A, B, C or D, and you are called upon to select the best answer and write the letter next to that answer on your answer paper – it is advisable to start answering each question in turn. There may be anywhere from 50 to 100 such questions in the three or four hours allotted and you can see how much time would be taken if you read through all the questions before beginning to answer any. Furthermore, if you come across a question or group of questions which you know would be difficult to answer, it would undoubtedly affect your handling of all the other questions.

4) If the examination is of the essay type and contains but a few questions, it is a moot point as to whether you should read all the questions before starting to answer any one. Of course, if you are given a choice – say five out of seven and the like – then it is essential to read all the questions so you can eliminate the two that are most difficult. If, however, you are asked to answer all the questions, there may be danger in trying to answer the easiest one first because you may find that you will spend too much time on it. The best technique is to answer the first question, then proceed to the second, etc.

5) Time your answers. Before the exam begins, write down the time it started, then add the time allowed for the examination and write down the time it must be completed, then divide the time available somewhat as follows:
   - If 3-1/2 hours are allowed, that would be 210 minutes. If you have 80 objective-type questions, that would be an average of 2-1/2 minutes per question. Allow yourself no more than 2 minutes per question, or a total of 160 minutes, which will permit about 50 minutes to review.
   - If for the time allotment of 210 minutes there are 7 essay questions to answer, that would average about 30 minutes a question. Give yourself only 25 minutes per question so that you have about 35 minutes to review.

6) The most important instruction is to *read each question* and make sure you know what is wanted. The second most important instruction is to *time yourself properly* so that you answer every question. The third most important instruction is to *answer every question*. Guess if you have to but include something for each question. Remember that you will receive no credit for a blank and will probably receive some credit if you write something in answer to an essay question. If you guess a letter – say "B" for a multiple-choice question – you may have guessed right. If you leave a blank as an answer to a multiple-choice question, the examiners may respect your feelings but it will not add a point to your score. Some exams may penalize you for wrong answers, so in such cases *only*, you may not want to guess unless you have some basis for your answer.

7) Suggestions
   a. Objective-type questions
      1. Examine the question booklet for proper sequence of pages and questions
      2. Read all instructions carefully
      3. Skip any question which seems too difficult; return to it after all other questions have been answered
      4. Apportion your time properly; do not spend too much time on any single question or group of questions

5. Note and underline key words – *all, most, fewest, least, best, worst, same, opposite*, etc.
6. Pay particular attention to negatives
7. Note unusual option, e.g., unduly long, short, complex, different or similar in content to the body of the question
8. Observe the use of "hedging" words – *probably, may, most likely*, etc.
9. Make sure that your answer is put next to the same number as the question
10. Do not second-guess unless you have good reason to believe the second answer is definitely more correct
11. Cross out original answer if you decide another answer is more accurate; do not erase until you are ready to hand your paper in
12. Answer all questions; guess unless instructed otherwise
13. Leave time for review

b. Essay questions
1. Read each question carefully
2. Determine exactly what is wanted. Underline key words or phrases.
3. Decide on outline or paragraph answer
4. Include many different points and elements unless asked to develop any one or two points or elements
5. Show impartiality by giving pros and cons unless directed to select one side only
6. Make and write down any assumptions you find necessary to answer the questions
7. Watch your English, grammar, punctuation and choice of words
8. Time your answers; don't crowd material

8) Answering the essay question

Most essay questions can be answered by framing the specific response around several key words or ideas. Here are a few such key words or ideas:

M's: manpower, materials, methods, money, management
P's: purpose, program, policy, plan, procedure, practice, problems, pitfalls, personnel, public relations

a. Six basic steps in handling problems:
1. Preliminary plan and background development
2. Collect information, data and facts
3. Analyze and interpret information, data and facts
4. Analyze and develop solutions as well as make recommendations
5. Prepare report and sell recommendations
6. Install recommendations and follow up effectiveness

b. Pitfalls to avoid
1. *Taking things for granted* – A statement of the situation does not necessarily imply that each of the elements is necessarily true; for example, a complaint may be invalid and biased so that all that can be taken for granted is that a complaint has been registered

2. *Considering only one side of a situation* – Wherever possible, indicate several alternatives and then point out the reasons you selected the best one
3. *Failing to indicate follow up* – Whenever your answer indicates action on your part, make certain that you will take proper follow-up action to see how successful your recommendations, procedures or actions turn out to be
4. *Taking too long in answering any single question* – Remember to time your answers properly

IX. AFTER THE TEST

Scoring procedures differ in detail among civil service jurisdictions although the general principles are the same. Whether the papers are hand-scored or graded by machine we have described, they are nearly always graded by number. That is, the person who marks the paper knows only the number – never the name – of the applicant. Not until all the papers have been graded will they be matched with names. If other tests, such as training and experience or oral interview ratings have been given, scores will be combined. Different parts of the examination usually have different weights. For example, the written test might count 60 percent of the final grade, and a rating of training and experience 40 percent. In many jurisdictions, veterans will have a certain number of points added to their grades.

After the final grade has been determined, the names are placed in grade order and an eligible list is established. There are various methods for resolving ties between those who get the same final grade – probably the most common is to place first the name of the person whose application was received first. Job offers are made from the eligible list in the order the names appear on it. You will be notified of your grade and your rank as soon as all these computations have been made. This will be done as rapidly as possible.

People who are found to meet the requirements in the announcement are called "eligibles." Their names are put on a list of eligible candidates. An eligible's chances of getting a job depend on how high he stands on this list and how fast agencies are filling jobs from the list.

When a job is to be filled from a list of eligibles, the agency asks for the names of people on the list of eligibles for that job. When the civil service commission receives this request, it sends to the agency the names of the three people highest on this list. Or, if the job to be filled has specialized requirements, the office sends the agency the names of the top three persons who meet these requirements from the general list.

The appointing officer makes a choice from among the three people whose names were sent to him. If the selected person accepts the appointment, the names of the others are put back on the list to be considered for future openings.

That is the rule in hiring from all kinds of eligible lists, whether they are for typist, carpenter, chemist, or something else. For every vacancy, the appointing officer has his choice of any one of the top three eligibles on the list. This explains why the person whose name is on top of the list sometimes does not get an appointment when some of the persons lower on the list do. If the appointing officer chooses the second or third eligible, the No. 1 eligible does not get a job at once, but stays on the list until he is appointed or the list is terminated.

X. HOW TO PASS THE INTERVIEW TEST

The examination for which you applied requires an oral interview test. You have already taken the written test and you are now being called for the interview test – the final part of the formal examination.

You may think that it is not possible to prepare for an interview test and that there are no procedures to follow during an interview. Our purpose is to point out some things you can do in advance that will help you and some good rules to follow and pitfalls to avoid while you are being interviewed.

What is an interview supposed to test?

The written examination is designed to test the technical knowledge and competence of the candidate; the oral is designed to evaluate intangible qualities, not readily measured otherwise, and to establish a list showing the relative fitness of each candidate – as measured against his competitors – for the position sought. Scoring is not on the basis of "right" and "wrong," but on a sliding scale of values ranging from "not passable" to "outstanding." As a matter of fact, it is possible to achieve a relatively low score without a single "incorrect" answer because of evident weakness in the qualities being measured.

Occasionally, an examination may consist entirely of an oral test – either an individual or a group oral. In such cases, information is sought concerning the technical knowledges and abilities of the candidate, since there has been no written examination for this purpose. More commonly, however, an oral test is used to supplement a written examination.

Who conducts interviews?

The composition of oral boards varies among different jurisdictions. In nearly all, a representative of the personnel department serves as chairman. One of the members of the board may be a representative of the department in which the candidate would work. In some cases, "outside experts" are used, and, frequently, a businessman or some other representative of the general public is asked to serve. Labor and management or other special groups may be represented. The aim is to secure the services of experts in the appropriate field.

However the board is composed, it is a good idea (and not at all improper or unethical) to ascertain in advance of the interview who the members are and what groups they represent. When you are introduced to them, you will have some idea of their backgrounds and interests, and at least you will not stutter and stammer over their names.

What should be done before the interview?

While knowledge about the board members is useful and takes some of the surprise element out of the interview, there is other preparation which is more substantive. It *is* possible to prepare for an oral interview – in several ways:

1) Keep a copy of your application and review it carefully before the interview

This may be the only document before the oral board, and the starting point of the interview. Know what education and experience you have listed there, and the sequence and dates of all of it. Sometimes the board will ask you to review the highlights of your experience for them; you should not have to hem and haw doing it.

2) Study the class specification and the examination announcement

Usually, the oral board has one or both of these to guide them. The qualities, characteristics or knowledges required by the position sought are stated in these documents. They offer valuable clues as to the nature of the oral interview. For example, if the job involves supervisory responsibilities, the announcement will usually indicate that knowledge of modern supervisory methods and the qualifications of the candidate as a supervisor will be tested. If so, you can expect such questions, frequently in the form of a hypothetical situation which you are expected to solve. NEVER go into an oral without knowledge of the duties and responsibilities of the job you seek.

3) Think through each qualification required

Try to visualize the kind of questions you would ask if you were a board member. How well could you answer them? Try especially to appraise your own knowledge and background in each area, *measured against the job sought*, and identify any areas in which you are weak. Be critical and realistic – do not flatter yourself.

4) Do some general reading in areas in which you feel you may be weak

For example, if the job involves supervision and your past experience has NOT, some general reading in supervisory methods and practices, particularly in the field of human relations, might be useful. Do NOT study agency procedures or detailed manuals. The oral board will be testing your understanding and capacity, not your memory.

5) Get a good night's sleep and watch your general health and mental attitude

You will want a clear head at the interview. Take care of a cold or any other minor ailment, and of course, no hangovers.

What should be done on the day of the interview?

Now comes the day of the interview itself. Give yourself plenty of time to get there. Plan to arrive somewhat ahead of the scheduled time, particularly if your appointment is in the fore part of the day. If a previous candidate fails to appear, the board might be ready for you a bit early. By early afternoon an oral board is almost invariably behind schedule if there are many candidates, and you may have to wait. Take along a book or magazine to read, or your application to review, but leave any extraneous material in the waiting room when you go in for your interview. In any event, relax and compose yourself.

The matter of dress is important. The board is forming impressions about you – from your experience, your manners, your attitude, and your appearance. Give your personal appearance careful attention. Dress your best, but not your flashiest. Choose conservative, appropriate clothing, and be sure it is immaculate. This is a business interview, and your appearance should indicate that you regard it as such. Besides, being well groomed and properly dressed will help boost your confidence.

Sooner or later, someone will call your name and escort you into the interview room. *This is it*. From here on you are on your own. It is too late for any more preparation. But remember, you asked for this opportunity to prove your fitness, and you are here because your request was granted.

What happens when you go in?

The usual sequence of events will be as follows: The clerk (who is often the board stenographer) will introduce you to the chairman of the oral board, who will introduce you to the other members of the board. Acknowledge the introductions before you sit down. Do not be surprised if you find a microphone facing you or a stenotypist sitting by. Oral interviews are usually recorded in the event of an appeal or other review.

Usually the chairman of the board will open the interview by reviewing the highlights of your education and work experience from your application – primarily for the benefit of the other members of the board, as well as to get the material into the record. Do not interrupt or comment unless there is an error or significant misinterpretation; if that is the case, do not hesitate. But do not quibble about insignificant matters. Also, he will usually ask you some question about your education, experience or your present job – partly to get you to start talking and to establish the interviewing "rapport." He may start the actual questioning, or turn it over to one of the other members. Frequently, each member undertakes the questioning on a particular area, one in which he is perhaps most competent, so you can expect each member to participate in the examination. Because time is limited, you may also expect some rather abrupt switches in the direction the questioning takes, so do not be upset by it. Normally, a board member will not pursue a single line of questioning unless he discovers a particular strength or weakness.

After each member has participated, the chairman will usually ask whether any member has any further questions, then will ask you if you have anything you wish to add. Unless you are expecting this question, it may floor you. Worse, it may start you off on an extended, extemporaneous speech. The board is not usually seeking more information. The question is principally to offer you a last opportunity to present further qualifications or to indicate that you have nothing to add. So, if you feel that a significant qualification or characteristic has been overlooked, it is proper to point it out in a sentence or so. Do not compliment the board on the thoroughness of their examination – they have been sketchy, and you know it. If you wish, merely say, "No thank you, I have nothing further to add." This is a point where you can "talk yourself out" of a good impression or fail to present an important bit of information. Remember, *you close the interview yourself.*

The chairman will then say, "That is all, Mr. _____, thank you." Do not be startled; the interview is over, and quicker than you think. Thank him, gather your belongings and take your leave. Save your sigh of relief for the other side of the door.

How to put your best foot forward

Throughout this entire process, you may feel that the board individually and collectively is trying to pierce your defenses, seek out your hidden weaknesses and embarrass and confuse you. Actually, this is not true. They are obliged to make an appraisal of your qualifications for the job you are seeking, and they want to see you in your best light. Remember, they must interview all candidates and a non-cooperative candidate may become a failure in spite of their best efforts to bring out his qualifications. Here are 15 suggestions that will help you:

1) Be natural – Keep your attitude confident, not cocky

If you are not confident that you can do the job, do not expect the board to be. Do not apologize for your weaknesses, try to bring out your strong points. The board is interested in a positive, not negative, presentation. Cockiness will antagonize any board member and make him wonder if you are covering up a weakness by a false show of strength.

2) Get comfortable, but don't lounge or sprawl

Sit erectly but not stiffly. A careless posture may lead the board to conclude that you are careless in other things, or at least that you are not impressed by the importance of the occasion. Either conclusion is natural, even if incorrect. Do not fuss with your clothing, a pencil or an ashtray. Your hands may occasionally be useful to emphasize a point; do not let them become a point of distraction.

3) Do not wisecrack or make small talk

This is a serious situation, and your attitude should show that you consider it as such. Further, the time of the board is limited – they do not want to waste it, and neither should you.

4) Do not exaggerate your experience or abilities

In the first place, from information in the application or other interviews and sources, the board may know more about you than you think. Secondly, you probably will not get away with it. An experienced board is rather adept at spotting such a situation, so do not take the chance.

5) If you know a board member, do not make a point of it, yet do not hide it

Certainly you are not fooling him, and probably not the other members of the board. Do not try to take advantage of your acquaintanceship – it will probably do you little good.

6) Do not dominate the interview

Let the board do that. They will give you the clues – do not assume that you have to do all the talking. Realize that the board has a number of questions to ask you, and do not try to take up all the interview time by showing off your extensive knowledge of the answer to the first one.

7) Be attentive

You only have 20 minutes or so, and you should keep your attention at its sharpest throughout. When a member is addressing a problem or question to you, give him your undivided attention. Address your reply principally to him, but do not exclude the other board members.

8) Do not interrupt

A board member may be stating a problem for you to analyze. He will ask you a question when the time comes. Let him state the problem, and wait for the question.

9) Make sure you understand the question

Do not try to answer until you are sure what the question is. If it is not clear, restate it in your own words or ask the board member to clarify it for you. However, do not haggle about minor elements.

10) Reply promptly but not hastily

A common entry on oral board rating sheets is "candidate responded readily," or "candidate hesitated in replies." Respond as promptly and quickly as you can, but do not jump to a hasty, ill-considered answer.

11) Do not be peremptory in your answers

A brief answer is proper – but do not fire your answer back. That is a losing game from your point of view. The board member can probably ask questions much faster than you can answer them.

12) Do not try to create the answer you think the board member wants

He is interested in what kind of mind you have and how it works – not in playing games. Furthermore, he can usually spot this practice and will actually grade you down on it.

13) Do not switch sides in your reply merely to agree with a board member

Frequently, a member will take a contrary position merely to draw you out and to see if you are willing and able to defend your point of view. Do not start a debate, yet do not surrender a good position. If a position is worth taking, it is worth defending.

14) Do not be afraid to admit an error in judgment if you are shown to be wrong

The board knows that you are forced to reply without any opportunity for careful consideration. Your answer may be demonstrably wrong. If so, admit it and get on with the interview.

15) Do not dwell at length on your present job

The opening question may relate to your present assignment. Answer the question but do not go into an extended discussion. You are being examined for a *new* job, not your present one. As a matter of fact, try to phrase ALL your answers in terms of the job for which you are being examined.

Basis of Rating

Probably you will forget most of these "do's" and "don'ts" when you walk into the oral interview room. Even remembering them all will not ensure you a passing grade. Perhaps you did not have the qualifications in the first place. But remembering them will help you to put your best foot forward, without treading on the toes of the board members.

Rumor and popular opinion to the contrary notwithstanding, an oral board wants you to make the best appearance possible. They know you are under pressure – but they also want to see how you respond to it as a guide to what your reaction would be under the pressures of the job you seek. They will be influenced by the degree of poise you display, the personal traits you show and the manner in which you respond.

ABOUT THIS BOOK

This book contains tests divided into Examination Sections. Go through each test, answering every question in the margin. We have also attached a sample answer sheet at the back of the book that can be removed and used. At the end of each test look at the answer key and check your answers. On the ones you got wrong, look at the right answer choice and learn. Do not fill in the answers first. Do not memorize the questions and answers, but understand the answer and principles involved. On your test, the questions will likely be different from the samples. Questions are changed and new ones added. If you understand these past questions you should have success with any changes that arise. Tests may consist of several types of questions. We have additional books on each subject should more study be advisable or necessary for you. Finally, the more you study, the better prepared you will be. This book is intended to be the last thing you study before you walk into the examination room. Prior study of relevant texts is also recommended. NLC publishes some of these in our Fundamental Series. Knowledge and good sense are important factors in passing your exam. Good luck also helps. So now study this Passbook, absorb the material contained within and take that knowledge into the examination. Then do your best to pass that exam.

EXAMINATION SECTION

EXAMINATION SECTION
TEST 1

DIRECTIONS: Each question or incomplete statement is followed by several suggested answers or completions. Select the one that BEST answers the question or completes the statement. *PRINT THE LETTER OF THE CORRECT ANSWER IN THE SPACE AT THE RIGHT.*

1. A bit is held in a hand drill by means of a(n)

    A. arbor B. chuck C. collet D. clamp

    1.____

2. The type of screw that MOST often requires a countersunk hole is a _____ head.

    A. flat B. round C. fillister D. hexagon

    2.____

3. Instead of using the ordinary 1 piece screwdriver, a screwdriver bit is MOST often used with a brace because of the

    A. increased length of the brace
    B. different types of bits available
    C. increased leverage of the brace
    D. ability to work in tight corners

    3.____

4. A thread gage is usually used to measure the

    A. thickness of a thread
    B. diameter of a thread
    C. number of threads per inch
    D. height of a thread

    4.____

5. The wheel of a glass cutter is BEST lubricated with

    A. kerosene
    B. linseed oil
    C. varnolene
    D. diesel oil

    5.____

6. A nail set is a

    A. group of nails of the same size and type
    B. group of nails of different sizes but the same type
    C. tool used to extract nails
    D. tool used to drive nails below the surface of wood

    6.____

7. To test for leaks in a gas line, it is BEST to use

    A. a match
    B. soapy water
    C. a colored dye
    D. ammonia

    7.____

8. Routing is the process of cutting a

    A. strip out of sheet metal
    B. groove in wood
    C. chamfer on a shaft
    D. core out of concrete

    8.____

9. A hacksaw frame has a wing nut mainly to

    A. make it easier to replace blades
    B. increase the strength of the frame
    C. prevent vibration of the blade
    D. adjust the length of the frame

    9.____

10. A mitre box is usually used with a _____ saw.

    A. hack   B. crosscut   C. rip   D. back

11. A continuous flexible saw blade is MOST often used on a _____ saw.

    A. radial   B. band   C. swing   D. table

12. A pipe reamer is used to

    A. clean out a length of pipe
    B. thread pipe
    C. remove burrs from the ends of pipe
    D. seal pipe joints

13. To lay out a straight cut on a piece of wood at the same angle as the cut on a second piece of wood, the PROPER tool to use is a

    A. bevel   B. cope   C. butt gauge   D. clevis

14. Before drilling a hole in a piece of metal, an indentation should be made with a _____ punch.

    A. pin   B. taper   C. center   D. drift

15. Curved cuts in wood are BEST made with a _____ saw.

    A. jig   B. veneer   C. radial   D. swing

16. A face plate is generally used to

    A. hold material while working with it on a lathe
    B. smooth out irregularities in a metal plate
    C. protect the finish on a metal plate
    D. locate centers of holes to be drilled on a drill press

17. A die would be used to

    A. gage the groove in a splined shaft
    B. cut a thread on a metal rod
    C. hold a piece to be machined on a milling machine
    D. control the depth of a hole to be drilled in a piece of metal

18. Before using a ladle to scoop up molten solder, you should make sure that the ladle is dry.
    This is done to prevent

    A. the solder from sticking to the ladle
    B. impurities from getting into the solder
    C. injuries due to splashing solder
    D. cooling of the solder

19. To PROPERLY adjust the gap on a spark plug, you should use a(n)   19.____
    A. inside caliper   B. center gauge
    C. wire type feeler gauge D. micrometer

20. The length of the MOST common type of folding wood rule is _____ feet.   20.____
    A. 4   B. 5   C. 6   D. 7

21. A four-foot mason's level is usually used to determine whether the top of a wall is level and whether it is   21.____
    A. square   B. plumb   C. rigid   D. in line

22. To match a tongue in a board, the matching board MUST have a   22.____
    A. rabbet   B. chamfer   C. bead   D. groove

23. When driving screws in close quarters, the BEST type of screwdriver to use is a(n)   23.____
    A. Phillips   B. offset   C. butt   D. angled

24. The term 12-24 refers to a _____ screw.   24.____
    A. wood   B. lag
    C. sheet metal   D. machine

25. To measure the length of a curved line on a drawing or plan, the PROPER tool to use in addition to a ruler is(are)   25.____
    A. dividers   B. calipers
    C. surface gage D. radius gage

26. For the standard machine screw, the diameter of a tap drill is generally   26.____
    A. *equal* to the diameter of the shaft of the screw at the base of the threads (the root diameter)
    B. *larger* than the root diameter, but smaller than the diameter of the screw
    C. *equal* to the diameter of the screw
    D. *larger* than the diameter of the screw

27. In order to drill a 1" hole accurately with a drill press, you should   27.____
    A. drill at high speeds
    B. use very little pressure on the drill
    C. drill partway down, release pressure on the drill, and then continue drilling
    D. drill a pilot hole first

28. Before taking apart an electric motor to repair, punch marks are sometimes placed on the casing near each other.   28.____
    The MOST probable reason for doing this is to
    A. make sure the parts lock together on reassembly
    B. properly line up the parts that are next to each other
    C. keep track of the number of parts in the assembly
    D. identify all the parts as coming from the one motor

29. To locate a point on a floor directly under a point on the ceiling, the PROPER tool to use is a

   A. square
   B. line level
   C. height gage
   D. plumb bob

Question 30.

DIRECTIONS: Question 30 is based on the diagram appearing below.

30. In the above diagram, the full P required to lift the weight a distance of four feet is MOST NEARLY _____ lbs.

   A. 50   B. 67   C. 75   D. 100

31. The EASIEST tool to use to determine whether the edge of a board is at right angles to the face of the board is a

   A. rafter square
   B. try square
   C. protractor
   D. marking gage

32. *Whetting* refers to

   A. tempering of tools by dipping them in water
   B. annealing of tools by heating and slow cooling
   C. brazing of carbide tips on tools
   D. sharpening of tools

33. The MOST difficult part of a plank to plane is the

   A. face   B. side   C. end   D. back

34. To prevent wood from splitting when drilling with an auger, it is BEST to

   A. use even pressure on the bit
   B. drill at a slow speed
   C. hold the wood tightly in a vise
   D. back up the wood with a piece of scrap wood

35. The term *dressing a grinding wheel* refers to 35.____

   A. setting up the wheel on the arbor
   B. restoring the sharpness of a wheel face that has become clogged
   C. placing flanges against the sides of the wheel
   D. bringing the wheel up to speed before using it

36. Heads of rivets are BEST cut off with a 36.____

   A. hacksaw   B. cold chisel
   C. fly cutter   D. reamer

37. A *V-block* is especially useful to 37.____

   A. prevent damage to work held in a vise
   B. hold round stock while a hole is being drilled into it
   C. prevent rolling of round stock stored on the ground
   D. shim up the end of a machine so that it is level

38. A full set of taps for a given size usually consists of a _____ tap. 38.____

   A. taper and bottoming
   B. taper and plug
   C. plug and bottoming
   D. taper, plug, and bottoming

39. Round thread cutting dies are usually held in stock by means of 39.____

   A. wing nuts   B. clamps   C. set screws   D. bolts

40. The one of the following diagrams that shows the plan view and the elevation of a counterbored hole is 40.____

A.

B.

C.

D.

41. With regard to pipe, *I.D.* usually means 41.____

   A. inside diameter   B. inside dressed
   C. invert diameter   D. installation date

42. A compression fitting is MOST often used to 42._____

   A. lubricate a wheel
   B. join two pieces of tubing
   C. reduce the diameter of a hole
   D. press fit a gear to a shaft

43. The shape of a mill file is basically 43._____

   A. flat   B. half round   C. triangular   D. square

44. Of the following, the ratio of tin to lead that will produce the solder with the LOWEST melting point is 44._____

   A. 30-70   B. 40-60   C. 50-50   D. 60-40

45. A safe edge on a file is one that 45._____

   A. is smooth and can not cut
   B. has a finer cut than the face of the file
   C. is rounded to prevent scratches
   D. has a coarser cut than the face of the file

46. The MOST frequent use of a file card is to _____ files. 46._____

   A. sort out   B. clean
   C. prevent damage to   D. prevent clogging of

47. The BEST way of determining whether a grinding wheel has an internal crack is to 47._____

   A. run the wheel at high speed, stop it, and examine the wheel
   B. spray lubricating oil on the sides of the wheel and check the amount of absorption of the oil
   C. hit the wheel with a rubber hammer and listen to the sound
   D. drop the wheel sharply on a table and then check the wheel

48. If a grinding wheel has worn to a smaller diameter, the BEST practice to follow is to 48._____

   A. discard the wheel
   B. continue using the wheel as before
   C. use the wheel, but at a faster speed
   D. use the wheel, but at a slower speed

49. With respect to the ordinary awl, 49._____

   A. only the tip is hardened
   B. the entire blade is hardened
   C. the tip is tempered, and the rest of the blade is hardened
   D. the entire blade is tempered

50. To prevent overheating of drills, it is BEST to use _____ oil. 50._____

   A. cutting   B. lubricating
   C. penetrating   D. heating

KEY (CORRECT ANSWERS)

1.	B	11.	B	21.	B	31.	B	41.	A
2.	A	12.	C	22.	D	32.	D	42.	B
3.	C	13.	A	23.	B	33.	C	43.	A
4.	C	14.	C	24.	D	34.	D	44.	D
5.	A	15.	A	25.	A	35.	B	45.	A
6.	D	16.	A	26.	B	36.	B	46.	B
7.	B	17.	B	27.	D	37.	B	47.	C
8.	B	18.	C	28.	B	38.	D	48.	C
9.	A	19.	C	29.	D	39.	C	49.	A
10.	D	20.	C	30.	D	40.	A	50.	A

TEST 2

DIRECTIONS: Each question or incomplete statement is followed by several suggested answers or completions. Select the one that BEST answers the question or completes the statement. *PRINT THE LETTER OF THE CORRECT ANSWER IN THE SPACE AT THE RIGHT.*

1. Crocus cloth is commonly used to   1._____

   A. protect finely machined surfaces from damage while the machines are being repaired
   B. remove rust from steel
   C. protect floors and furniture while painting walls
   D. wipe up oil and grease that has spilled

2. Before using a new paint brush, the FIRST operation should be to   2._____

   A. remove loose bristles
   B. soak the brush in linseed oil
   C. hang the brush up overnight
   D. clean the brush with turpentine

3. When sharpening a hand saw, the FIRST operation is to   3._____

   A. file the teeth down to the same height
   B. shape the teeth to the proper profile
   C. bend the teeth over to provide clearance when sawing
   D. clean the gullies with a file

4. To prevent solder from dripping when soldering a vertical seam, it is BEST to   4._____

   A. hold a waxed rag under the soldering iron
   B. use the soldering iron in a horizontal position
   C. tin the soldering iron on one side only
   D. solder the seam in the order from bottom to top

5. If a round nut has two holes in the face, the PROPER type wrench to use to tighten this nut is a(n)   5._____

   A. Stillson   B. monkey   C. spanner   D. open end

6. A box wrench is BEST used on   6._____

   A. pipe fittings   B. flare nuts
   C. hexagonal nuts   D. Allen screws

7. To prevent damage to fine finishes on metal work that is to be held in a vise, you should   7._____

   A. clamp the work lightly
   B. use brass inserts on the vise
   C. wrap the work with cloth before inserting it in the vise
   D. substitute a smooth face plate for the serrated plate on the vise

8. The MOST frequent use for a turnbuckle is to

   A. tighten a guy wire
   B. adjust shims on a machine
   C. bolt a bracket to a wall
   D. support electric cable from a ceiling

9. To form the head of a tinner's rivet, the PROPER tool to use is a rivet

   A. anvil   B. plate   C. set   D. brake

10. A socket speed handle MOST closely resembles a

    A. screwdriver   B. brace   C. spanner   D. spin grip

11. Tips of masonry drills are usually made of

    A. steel   B. carbide   C. corundum   D. monel

12. The BEST flux to use for soldering galvanized iron is

    A. resin
    B. sal ammoniac
    C. borax
    D. muriatic acid

13. The one of the following that is NOT a common type of oilstone is

    A. silicon carbide
    B. aluminum oxide
    C. hard Arkansas
    D. pumice

14. A method of joining metals using temperatures intermediate between soldering and welding is

    A. corbelling   B. brazing   C. annealing   D. lapping

15. When an unusually high degree of accuracy is required with woodwork, lines should be marked with a

    A. pencil ground to a chisel point
    B. pencil line over a crayon line
    C. sharp knife point
    D. scriber

16. The MOST important difference between pipe threads and V threads on bolts is that pipe threads are usually

    A. longer
    B. sharper
    C. tapered
    D. more evenly spaced

17. A street elbow differs from the ordinary elbow in that the street elbow has

    A. different diameter threads at each end
    B. male threads at one end and female threads at the other
    C. female threads at both ends
    D. male threads at both ends

18. Water hammer in a pipe line can MOST often be stopped by the installation of a(n)

    A. pressure reducing valve
    B. expansion joint
    C. flexible coupling
    D. air chamber

19. If water is leaking from the top part of a bibcock, the part that should be replaced is MOST likely the

    A. bibb washer   B. packing
    C. seat   D. bibb screw

20. When joining electric wires together in a fixture box, the BEST thing to use are wire

    A. connectors   B. couplings   C. clamps   D. bolts

21. If the name plate of a motor indicates that it is a split phase motor, it is LIKELY that this motor

    A. is a universal motor
    B. operates on DC only
    C. operates on AC only
    D. operates either on DC at full power or on AC at reduced power

22. To make driving of a screw into hard wood easier, it is BEST to lubricate the threads of the screw with

    A. varnoline   B. penetrating oil
    C. beeswax   D. cutting oil

23. Assume that a thermostatically controlled oil heater fails to operate. To determine whether it is the thermostat that is at fault, you should

    A. check the circuit breaker
    B. connect a wire across the terminals of the thermostat
    C. replace the contacts on the thermostat
    D. put an ammeter on the line

24. The function of the carburetor on a gasoline engine is to

    A. mix the air and gasoline properly
    B. filter the fuel
    C. filter the air to engine
    D. pump the gasoline into the cylinder

25. If a car owner complains that the battery in his car is constantly running dry, the item that should be checked FIRST is the

    A. fan belt   B. generator
    C. voltage regulator   D. relay

26. On MOST modern automobiles, foot brake pressure is transmitted to the brake drums by

    A. air pressure   B. mechanical linkage
    C. hydraulic fluid D. electro-magnetic force

27. Assume that the engine of a car remains cold even though it is run for a period of time. The part that is MOST likely at fault is the

    A. heat by-pass valve   B. thermostat
    C. heater control   D. choke

28. To permit easy stripping of concrete forms, they should be

    A. dried   B. oiled   C. wet down   D. cleaned

29. To prevent honey combing in concrete, the concrete should be

    A. vibrated
    B. cured
    C. heated in cold weather
    D. protected from the rain

30. The MAIN reason for using wire mesh in connection with concrete work is to

    A. strain the impurities from the sand
    B. increase the strength of the concrete
    C. hold the forms together
    D. protect the concrete till it hardens

31. Segregation of concrete is MOST often caused by pouring concrete

    A. in cold weather
    B. from too great a height
    C. too rapidly
    D. into a form in which the concrete has already begun to harden

32. Headers in carpentry are MOST closely associated with

    A. trimmers
    B. cantilevers
    C. posts
    D. newels

33. Joists are very often supported by

    A. suspenders
    B. base plates
    C. anchor bolts
    D. bridal irons

34. At outside corners, the type of joint MOST frequently used on a baseboard is the

    A. plowed
    B. mitered
    C. mortise and tenon
    D. butt

35. The vehicle used with latex paints is usually

    A. linseed oil
    B. shellac
    C. varnish
    D. water

36. *Boxing* of paint refers to the _____ of paints.

    A. mixing   B. storage   C. use   D. canning

37. When painting wood, nail holes should be puttied

    A. *before* applying the prime coat
    B. *after* applying the prime coat but before the second coat
    C. *after* applying the second coat but before the third coat
    D. *after* applying the third coat

38. In laying up a brick wall, you find that at the end of the wall there is not enough space for a full brick.
    You should use a

    A. stretcher   B. bat   C. corbel   D. bull nose

39. Pointing a brick wall is the same as

    A. truing up the wall
    B. topping the wall with a waterproof surface
    C. repairing the mortar joints in the wall
    D. providing a foundation for the wall

39.____

40. The pigment MOST often used in a prime coat of paint on steel to prevent rusting is

    A. lampblack
    B. calcimine
    C. zinc oxide
    D. red lead

40.____

41. If you find a co-worker lying unconscious across an electric wire, the FIRST thing you should do is

    A. get him off the wire
    B. call the foreman
    C. get a doctor
    D. shut off the power

41.____

42.

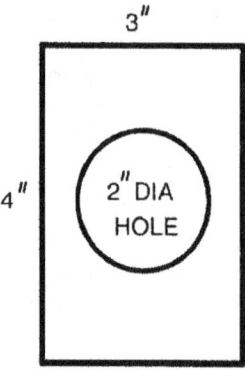

The area of the metal plate shown above, minus the hole area, is MOST NEARLY _____ square inches.

A. 8.5   B. 8.9   C. 9.4   D. 10.1

42.____

43.

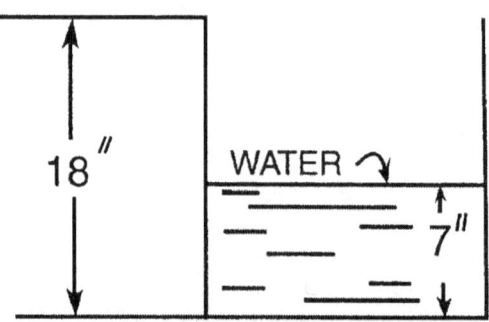

The percentage of the above tank that is filled with water is MOST NEARLY

A. 33   B. 35   C. 37   D. 39

43.____

44.

 TOP VIEW

 FRONT VIEW

The top and front view of an object are shown above. The right side view will MOST likely look like

A.    B.    C.    D.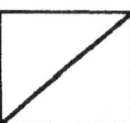

45.

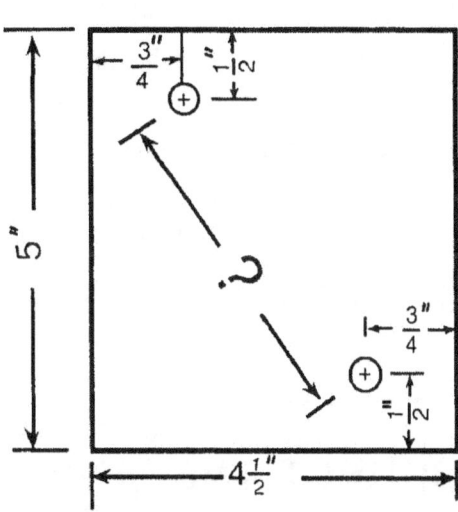

The distance between centers of the holes in the above diagram is MOST NEARLY

A. $4\frac{1}{2}"$ B. 4 3/4"   C. 5"   D. $5\frac{1}{4}"$

Questions 46-48.

DIRECTIONS: Questions 46 through 48, inclusive, are to be answered in accordance with the paragraph below.

A steam heating system with steam having a pressure of less than 10 pounds is called a low-pressure system. The majority of steam-heating systems are of this type. The steam may be provided by low-pressure boilers installed expressly for the purpose, or it may be gener-

ated in boilers at a higher pressure and reduced in pressure before admitted to the heating mains. In other instances, it may be possible to use exhaust steam which has been made to run engines and other machines and which still contains enough heat to be utilized in the heating system. The first case represents the system of heating used in the ordinary residence or other small building; the other two represent the systems of heating employed in industrial buildings where a power plant is installed for general power purposes.

46. According to the above paragraph, whether or not a steam heating system is considered a low pressure system is determined by the pressure   46.____

    A. generated by the boiler
    B. in the heating main
    C. at the inlet side of the reducing valve
    D. of the exhaust

47. According to the above paragraph, steam used for heating is sometimes obtained from steam   47.____

    A. generated principally to operate machinery
    B. exhausted from larger boilers
    C. generated at low pressure and brought up to high pressure before being used
    D. generated by engines other than boilers

48. As used in the above paragraph, the word *expressly* means   48.____

    A. rapidly   B. specifically
    C. usually   D. mainly

49. Of the following words, the one that is CORRECTLY spelled is   49.____

    A. suficient   B. sufficant
    C. sufficient   D. suficiant

50. Of the following words, the one that is CORRECTLY spelled is   50.____

    A. fairly   B. fairley   C. farely   D. fairlie

KEY (CORRECT ANSWERS)

1. B	11. B	21. C	31. B	41. D
2. A	12. D	22. C	32. A	42. B
3. A	13. D	23. B	33. D	43. D
4. C	14. B	24. A	34. B	44. A
5. C	15. C	25. C	35. D	45. C
6. C	16. C	26. C	36. A	46. B
7. B	17. B	27. B	37. B	47. A
8. A	18. D	28. B	38. B	48. B
9. C	19. B	29. A	39. C	49. C
10. B	20. A	30. B	40. D	50. A

EXAMINATION SECTION
TEST 1

DIRECTIONS: Each question or incomplete statement is followed by several suggested answers or completions. Select the one that BEST answers the question or completes the statement. *PRINT THE LETTER OF THE CORRECT ANSWER IN THE SPACE AT THE RIGHT.*

1. The composition of plumber's solder for wiping is APPROXIMATELY (ratio of tin to lead) 1._____

    A. 40-60   B. 50-50   C. 60-40   D. 70-30

2. A device used to lift sewage to the level of a sewer from a floor below the sewer grade is known as a(n) 2._____

    A. elevator   B. ejector   C. sump   D. conveyer

3. A check valve in a piping system will 3._____

    A. permit excessive pressures in a boiler
    B. eliminate water hammer
    C. permit water to flow in only one direction
    D. control the rate of flow of water

4. The chemical MOST frequently used to clean drains clogged with grease is 4._____

    A. muriatic acid   B. soda ash
    C. ammonia   D. caustic soda

5. To test for leaks in a newly installed C.I. waste stack, 5._____

    A. oil of peppermint is poured into the top of the stack
    B. smoke under pressure is pumped into the stack
    C. a water meter is used to measure the water flow
    D. dye is placed in the system at the top of the stack

6. When installing a catch basin, the outlet should be located 6._____

    A. at the same level as the inlet
    B. above the inlet
    C. below the inlet
    D. at the invert

7. The copper float in a low down water tank is perforated so that water enters the ball. As a result, the tank will 7._____

    A. flush once, and then will not operate again
    B. not flush at all
    C. not flush completely
    D. continue to flush, but water will be wasted

8. If water leaks from the stem of a faucet when the faucet is opened, the _____ should be 8._____

    A. faucet; replaced   B. cap nut; rethreaded
    C. seat; reground   D. packing; replaced

9. In a hot water heating system, it may be necessary to *bleed* radiators to

   A. relieve high steam pressure
   B. permit entrapped, air to escape
   C. allow condensate to return to the boiler
   D. drain off waste water

10. When painting raw wood, puttying of nail holes should be done

    A. 24 hours before the prime coat
    B. immediately before the prime coat
    C. after the prime coat and before the second coat
    D. after the second coat and before the finish

11. In general, the one of the following that will dry *tack free* in the SHORTEST time is

    A. lacquer   B. varnish   C. enamel   D. oil paint

12. The *vehicle* MOST frequently used in paints for exterior wood surfaces is

    A. white lead
    B. linseed oil
    C. japan
    D. varnish

13. Painting of an interior plastered wall is usually delayed until the plaster is dry. If this practice is NOT followed, the paint might

    A. chalk   B. fade   C. run   D. blister

14. A *sealer* applied over knots and pitch streaks to prevent *bleeding* through paint is

    A. shellac
    B. lacquer
    C. coal tar
    D. carnauba wax

15. Painting of outside steel in near freezing (32° F) weather is poor practice MAINLY because

    A. the paint will not dry properly
    B. ice will form in the thinner
    C. more paint is required
    D. paint fumes are dangerous

16. When repainting exterior woodwork that has a glossy finish, good adhesion of paint is BEST obtained by first

    A. *washing* the work with diluted lye
    B. *dulling* the work with sandpaper
    C. *warming* the work with an electric heater
    D. *roughening* the work with a rasp

17. The one of the following methods of cleaning steelwork prior to painting that is NOT commonly used on exterior work, such as bridges, is

    A. sandblasting
    B. flame cleaning
    C. wire brushing
    D. pickling

18. When spraying oil paints, the type of gun and nozzle preferred is a _____ feed gun, _____ mix nozzle.

    A. pressure; internal
    B. pressure; external
    C. syphon; internal
    D. syphon; external

19. When opening a bag of cement, you find that the cement is lumpy.
    The cement should be

    A. discarded and not used at all
    B. crushed before placing in the mixer
    C. used as is since the mixer will grind it
    D. well mixed with water and stored overnight before using

20. A 1:2:4 concrete mix by volume is specified.
    If 6 cubic feet of cement is to be used in the mix, the volume of sand to use is, in cubic feet,

    A. 3   B. 6   C. 12   D. 24

21. Honeycombing in concrete is BEST prevented by

    A. increasing water-cement ratio
    B. heating concrete in cold weather
    C. using mechanical vibrators
    D. adding calcium chloride

22. When a lightweight concrete is required, the one of the following that is COMMONLY used as an aggregate is

    A. gravel   B. brick chips   C. stone   D. cinders

23. A rubbed finish on concrete is USUALLY obtained by use of a

    A. carborundum brick
    B. garnet sanding belt
    C. fibre brush and wax
    D. pad of steel wool

24. A copper strip is frequently embedded in the concrete across a construction joint in a concrete wall.
    The purpose of this is to

    A. make a watertight joint
    B. bond the two parts of the wall together
    C. prevent unequal settlement
    D. retard temperature cracking

25. In brickwork laid in common bond, a header course USUALLY occurs in every _____ course.

    A. 2nd   B. 4th   C. 6th   D. 8th

26. Pointing of brickwork refers to

    A. cutting brick to fit
    B. patching mortar joints
    C. attaching brick veneer
    D. arranging brick in an arch

27. Furring is applied to brick walls to

    A. strengthen the wall
    B. waterproof the wall
    C. provide ventilation to prevent condensation
    D. provide a base for lathing

28. The FIRST coat in plaster work is *scratched* in order to

    A. remove excess plaster
    B. smooth the base for the second coat
    C. provide a bond for the second coat
    D. strengthen the base coat

29. An alloy used where resistance to corrosion is important is

    A. tungsten   B. mild steel   C. monel   D. tin

30. The size of iron pipe is given in terms of its nominal

    A. weight   B. inside diameter
    C. outside diameter   D. wall thickness

31. When preparing surfaces to be soldered, the FIRST step is

    A. tinning   B. sweating   C. heating   D. cleaning

32. To test for leaks in an acetylene torch, it is BEST that one use

    A. soapy water   B. a match
    C. a gas with a strong odor D. a pressure gauge

33. One advantage of using a Pittsburgh lock seam when joining two pieces of sheet metal is that, once formed in the shop, it may be assembled anywhere with a

    A. hickey   B. swage   C. template   D. mallet

34. White cast iron is

    A. hard and brittle   B. hard and ductile
    C. ductile and malleable D. brittle and malleable

35. The gage used for measuring copper wire is

    A. U.S. Standard   B. Stubbs
    C. Washburn and Moen   D. Brown and Sharpe

36. The BEST flux to use when soldering copper wires in an electric circuit is

    A. sal ammoniac   B. zinc chloride
    C. rosin   D. borax

37. The spark test, to determine the approximate composition of an unknown metal, is made by

    A. holding the metal against a grinding wheel
    B. striking flint on the unknown metal
    C. connecting wires from a source of electric power to the metal and striking an arc with a bare wire
    D. heating with an oxyacetylene torch

38. The one of the following metals that is MOST commonly used for bearings is 38.____

   A. duraluminum   B. brass   C. babbit   D. lead

39. A *tailstock* is found on a 39.____

   A. drill press   B. shaper   C. planer   D. lathe

40. The BEST lubricant to use when cutting screw threads in steel is 40.____

   A. naphtha   B. 3-in-1 oil
   C. lard oil   D. linseed oil

41. When a high speed cutting tool is required, the tip is frequently made of 41.____

   A. carborundum   B. tungsten carbide
   C. bronze   D. vanadium

42. A nut is turned on a 3/4"-10 bolt. 42.____
    When the nut is turned five complete turns on this bolt, the distance it moves along the bolt

   A. depends on the type of thread   B. is 0.2 inches
   C. is 0.375 inches   D. is 0.5 inches

43. Of the following, the STRONGEST screw thread form is the 43.____

   A. Whitworth   B. Acme
   C. National Standard   D. V

44. *Knurling* refers to 44.____

   A. rolling depressions in a fixed pattern on a cylindrical surface
   B. turning between centers on a lathe
   C. making deep cuts in a flat plate with a milling machine
   D. drilling matching holes in bolt and nut for a cotter pin

45. A special device used to guide the drill as well as to hold the work when drilling is known as a 45.____

   A. dolly   B. jig   C. chuck   D. collet

46. Tools that have a *Morse taper* would be used on a 46.____

   A. milling machine   B. shaper
   C. planer   D. drill press

47. When tapping a blind hole in a plate, the FIRST tap to use is a 47.____

   A. plug   B. bottoming   C. lead   D. taper

48. An important safety practice to remember when cutting a rivet with a chisel is to wear 48.____

   A. leather gloves   B. steel toe shoes
   C. cup goggles   D. a hard hat

49. Electricians working around *live wires* should wear gloves made of 49.____

    A. asbestos   B. metal mesh   C. leather   D. rubber

50. Storage of oily rags presents a safety hazard because of possible 50.____

    A. fire   B. poisonous flames
    C. attraction of rats   D. leakage of oil

KEY (CORRECT ANSWERS)

1.	A	11.	A	21.	C	31.	D	41.	B
2.	B	12.	B	22.	D	32.	A	42.	D
3.	C	13.	D	23.	A	33.	D	43.	B
4.	D	14.	A	24.	A	34.	A	44.	A
5.	B	15.	A	25.	C	35.	B	45.	B
6.	C	16.	B	26.	B	36.	C	46.	D
7.	D	17.	D	27.	D	37.	A	47.	D
8.	D	18.	A	28.	C	38.	C	48.	C
9.	B	19.	A	29.	C	39.	D	49.	D
10.	C	20.	C	30.	B	40.	C	50.	A

TEST 2

DIRECTIONS: Each question or incomplete statement is followed by several suggested answers or completions. Select the one that BEST answers the question or completes the statement. *PRINT THE LETTER OF THE CORRECT ANSWER IN THE SPACE AT THE RIGHT.*

1. *Shimmying* of the front wheels of a truck is MOST frequently caused by   1.____

    A. worn front brake drums
    B. a worn differential gear
    C. a loose steering gear
    D. a dead shock absorber

2. The MOST important reason for maintaining correct air pressure in all tires of a truck is to   2.____

    A. prevent the truck from swerving when brakes are applied
    B. permit the truck to stop quicker in an emergency
    C. provide a smoother ride
    D. prevent excessive wear on the tires

3. The oil gage on the dashboard of a truck indicates   3.____

    A. the amount of oil in the pan
    B. the pressure at which the oil is being pumped
    C. if the oil filter is working
    D. the temperature of the oil in the motor

4. An unbalanced wheel on a truck is corrected by   4.____

    A. bending the rim slightly
    B. adjusting the king pin
    C. changing the ratio of caster to camber
    D. adding small weights to the rim

5. A cold motor on a truck should be warmed up in wintertime by   5.____

    A. turning on the heater and pouring warm water into the radiator
    B. allowing the motor to idle for a few minutes
    C. racing the motor
    D. alternately pressing the gas pedal to the floor and releasing it

6. The brake pedal on a truck goes to the floorboard when pushed. The one of the following that would cause this condition is   6.____

    A. air in the hydraulic system
    B. wet brakes
    C. excessive fluid in the cylinders
    D. a loose backing plate

7. The ammeter of a truck indicates no charge during operation even though the battery is run down. To find the fault, the generator field terminal is grounded. The ammeter now shows a charge. The part that is defective is the   7.____

    A. generator field coil
    B. armature
    C. brushes
    D. voltage regulator

8. The part used to control the ratio of air and gasoline in a truck engine is the

   A. bogie   B. filter   C. carburetor   D. pump

9. The MAIN purpose of a vacuum booster on a truck engine is to

   A. increase the manifold vacuum
   B. assist windshield wiper operation
   C. provide a steadier fuel flow
   D. govern engine speed

10. The purpose of grounding the frame of an electric motor is to

    A. prevent excessive vibration
    B. eliminate shock hazards
    C. reduce power requirements
    D. prevent overheating

11. The one of the following that is NOT part of an electric motor is a

    A. brush   B. rheostat   C. pole   D. commutator

12. An electrical transformer would be used to

    A. change current from AC to DC
    B. raise or lower the power
    C. raise or lower the voltage
    D. change the frequency

13. The piece of equipment that would be rated in ampere hours is a

    A. storage battery
    B. bus bar
    C. rectifier
    D. capacitor

14. A ballast is a necessity in a(n)

    A. motor generator set
    B. fluorescent lighting system
    C. oil circuit breaker
    D. synchronous converter

15. The power factor in an AC circuit is on when

    A. no current is flowing
    B. the voltage at the source is a minimum
    C. the voltage and current are in phase
    D. there is no load

16.

    Neglecting the internal resistance in the battery, the current flowing through the battery shown in the sketch above is _____ amp.

    A. 3   B. 6   C. 9   D. 12

17. When excess current flows, a circuit breaker is opened directly by the action of a
    A. condenser   B. transistor   C. relay   D. solenoid

18. The MAIN purpose of bridging in building floor construction is to
    A. spread floor loads evenly to joists
    B. reduce the number of joists required
    C. permit use of thinner subflooring
    D. reduce noise passage through floors

19. Of the following, the material MOST commonly used for subflooring is
    A. rock lath   B. insulation board
    C. plywood   D. transite

20. In connection with stair construction, the one of the following that is LEAST related to the others is
    A. tread   B. cap   C. nosing   D. riser

21. The type of nail MOST commonly used in flooring is
    A. common   B. cut   C. brad   D. casing

22. The edge joint of flooring boards is COMMONLY
    A. mortise and tenon   B. shiplap
    C. half lap   D. tongue and groove

23. The purpose of a ridge board in building construction is to
    A. locate corners of a building
    B. keep plaster work smooth
    C. support the ends of roof rafters
    D. conceal openings at the eaves

24. To prevent splintering of wood when using an auger bit,
    A. the bit should be hollow ground
    B. hold the piece of wood in a vise
    C. clamp a piece of scrap wood to the back of the piece being drilled
    D. use a slow speed on the drill press

25. End grain of a post can be MOST easily planed by use of a _____ plane.
    A. rafter   B. jack   C. fore   D. block

26. A butt gauge is used when
    A. hanging doors   B. laying out stairs
    C. making rafter cuts   D. framing studs

27. The one of the following grades of sandpaper with the FINEST grit is
    A. 0   B. 2/0   C. 1/2   D. 1

28. The sum of the following numbers, 3 7/8, 14 1/4, 6 7/16, 22 3/16, 8 1/2 is   28.___

    A. 55 1/16   B. 55 1/8   C. 55 3/16   D. 55 1/4

29. The area of the rectangular field shown in the diagram at the right is, in square feet,   29.___

    A. 29,456
    B. 29,626
    C. 29,716
    D. 29,836

    437 FT.
    68 ft

30. The cost of material is approximately 3/8ths of the total cost of a certain job. If the total cost of the job is $127.56, then the cost of material is MOST NEARLY   30.___

    A. $47.83   B. $48.24   C. $48.65   D. $49.06

31. A blueprint is drawn to a scale of 1/4" = 1'0". A line on the blueprint that is not dimensioned is measured with a ruler and found to be 3 3/8" long.
    The length represented by this line is   31.___

    A. 13'2"   B. 13'4"   C. 13'6"   D. 13'8"

32. A maintainer, in repairing a brick wall, spends one-half hour getting materials, forty-three minutes chipping and cleaning the wall, fifteen minutes mixing the mortar, and one hour and twenty-seven minutes in applying the brick and finishing.
    The total time spent on this repair job is _____ hours _____ minute(s).   32.___

    A. 2; 45   B. 2; 50   C. 2; 55   D. 3; 0

33. *Employees are responsible for the good care, proper maintenance, and <u>serviceable condition</u> of property issued or assigned to their use.*
    As used above, *serviceable condition* means MOST NEARLY   33.___

    A. capable of being repaired   B. fit for use
    C. ease of handling   D. minimum cost

34. *An employee shall be on the alert constantly for potential accident hazards.*
    As used above, *potential* means MOST NEARLY   34.___

    A. dangerous   B. careless   C. possible   D. frequent

Questions 35-37.

DIRECTIONS: Questions 35 to 37, inclusive, are to be answered in accordance with the following paragraph.

All cement work contracts, more or less, in setting. The contraction in concrete walls and other structures causes fine cracks to develop at regular intervals. The tendency to contract increases in direct proportion to the quantity of cement in the concrete. A rich mixture will contract more than a lean mixture. A concrete wall, which has been made of a very lean mixture and which has been built by filling only about one foot in depth of concrete in the form each day will frequently require close inspection to reveal the cracks.

35. According to the above paragraph,

    A. shrinkage seldom occurs in concrete
    B. shrinkage occurs only in certain types of concrete
    C. by placing concrete at regular intervals, shrinkage may be avoided
    D. it is impossible to prevent shrinkage

36. According to the above paragraph, the one of the factors which reduces shrinkage in concrete is the

    A. volume of concrete in wall
    B. height of each day's pour
    C. length of wall
    D. length and height of wall

37. According to the above paragraph, a rich mixture

    A. pours the easiest
    B. shows the largest amount of cracks
    C. is low in cement content
    D. need not be inspected since cracks are few

Questions 38-39.

DIRECTIONS: Questions 38 and 39 are to be answered in accordance with the following paragraph.

Painting is done to preserve surfaces, and unless the surface is properly prepared, good preservation will not be possible. Apply paint only to clean dry surfaces. After a surface has been scaled, which means that all loose paint and rust are removed by chipping, scraping, and wire brushing, be sure all dust and dirt are completely removed.

38. According to the above paragraph, the MAIN purpose of painting a wall is to _____ the wall.

    A. clean   B. waterproof
    C. protect   D. remove dust from

39. According to the above paragraph,

    A. chipping, scraping, and wire brushing are the only methods permitted for cleaning surfaces
    B. painting is effective only when the surface is clean
    C. scaling refers only to the removal of rust
    D. paint may be applied on wet surfaces

40. The order in which the dimensions of stock are listed on a bill of materials is

    A. thickness, length, and width   B. thickness, width, and length
    C. width, length, and thickness   D. length, thickness, and width

41. The glue that will BEST withstand extreme exposure to moisture and water is _____ glue.

   A. polyvinyl   B. resorcinol
   C. powdered resin   D. protein

42. Four board feet of lumber, listed at $350.00 per M, will cost

   A. $3.50   B. $1.40   C. $1.30   D. $4.00

43. The cap iron or chip breaker stiffens the plane iron and

   A. protects the cutting edge
   B. curls the shaving
   C. regulates the thickness of the shaving
   D. reduces mouth gap

44. Coping-saw blades have teeth shaped like those on a _____ saw.

   A. dovetail   B. crosscut   C. back   D. rip

45. Of the following, the claw hammer that is BEST suited for general use in a woodworking shop is the _____ claw.

   A. straight   B. bell-faced curved
   C. plain-faced curved D. adze eye curved

46. The natural binder which cements wood fibers together and makes wood solid is

   A. cellulose   B. lignin
   C. alpha-cellulose D. trichocarpa

47. The plane that is BEST suited for trimming the bottom of a dado or lap joint is the _____ plane.

   A. block   B. router   C. rabbet   D. core-box

48. Brads are fasteners that are similar to _____ nails.

   A. escutcheon   B. box
   C. finishing   D. duplex head

49. The plane in which the plane iron is inserted with its bevel in the up position is the _____ plane.

   A. fore   B. rabbet   C. block   D. circular

50. Coating materials used to protect wood against fire USUALLY contain a water soluble fire-retardant such as

   A. ammonium chloride B. sodium perborate
   C. sodium silicate   D. sal soda

KEY (CORRECT ANSWERS)

1. C	11. B	21. B	31. C	41. B
2. D	12. C	22. D	32. C	42. B
3. B	13. A	23. C	33. B	43. B
4. D	14. B	24. C	34. C	44. D
5. B	15. C	25. D	35. D	45. B
6. A	16. A	26. A	36. B	46. B
7. D	17. D	27. B	37. B	47. B
8. C	18. A	28. D	38. C	48. C
9. B	19. C	29. C	39. B	49. C
10. B	20. B	30. A	40. B	50. C

EXAMINATION SECTION
TEST 1

DIRECTIONS: Each question or incomplete statement is followed by several suggested answers or completions. Select the one that BEST answers the question or completes the statement. *PRINT THE LETTER OF THE CORRECT ANSWER IN THE SPACE AT THE RIGHT.*

Questions 1-8.

DIRECTIONS: Questions 1 through 8 involve tests on the fuse box arrangement shown below. All tests are to be performed with a neon tester or a lamp test bank consisting of two 6-watt, 120-volt lamps connected in series. Do not make any assumptions about the conditions of the circuits. Draw your conclusions only from the information obtained with the neon tester or the two-lamp test bank, applied to the circuits as called for.

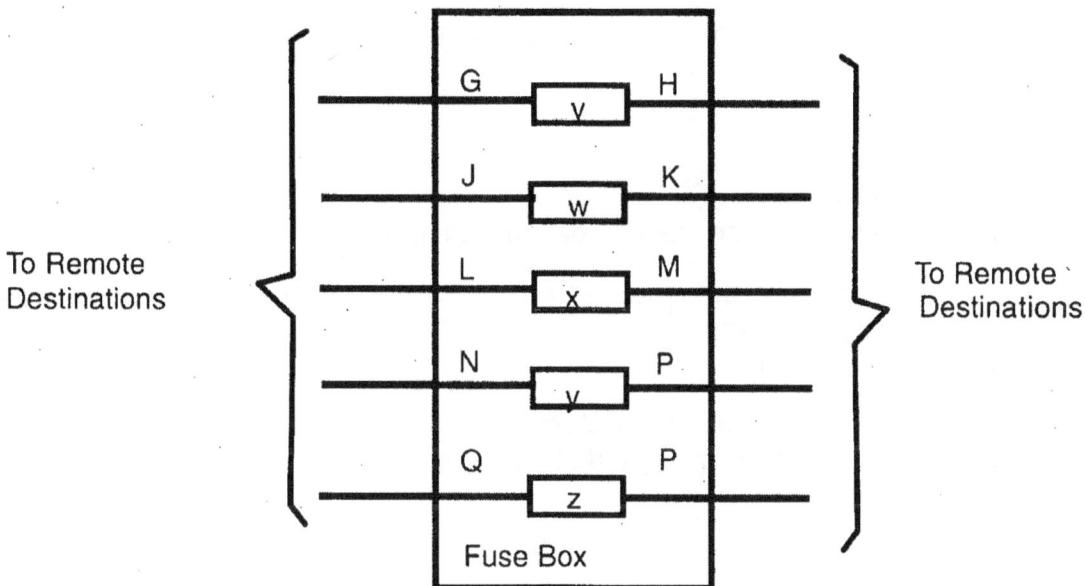

1. The two lamp test bank is placed from point G to joint J, and both lamps light. One of the lamps is momentarily removed from its socket; during that instant, the other lamp in the series-connected test bank should

   A. go dark
   B. get dimmer
   C. remain at same brightness
   D. get brighter

2. The test bank with two 60-watt, 120-volt lamps in series should be used on circuits with

   A. wattages only from 60 to 120 watts
   B. wattages only from 0 to 120 watts
   C. voltages only from 120 to 240 volts
   D. voltages only from 0 to 240 volts

29

3. The neon tester is placed from point G to point J and only one-half of the neon tester lights.
   It should be concluded that

   A. half of the tester has gone bad
   B. a wire has become disconnected in the circuit
   C. the voltage is AC
   D. the voltage is DC

4. If both lamps in the test bank light when placed directly across one of the above fuses, it should be concluded that

   A. the fuse is good
   B. the fuse is blown
   C. the fuse is overrated
   D. further tests have to be made to determine the condition of the fuse

5. If the lamp test bank does not light when placed directly across one of the above fuses, it should be concluded that

   A. the fuse is good
   B. the fuse is blown
   C. the fuse is overrated
   D. further tests have to be made to determine the condition of the fuse

6. The lamp test bank lights when placed from point G to point J but does not light when placed from point H to point J.
   It should be concluded that

   A. the wire to point H has become disconnected
   B. the wire to point J has become disconnected
   C. fuse v is bad
   D. fuse w is bad

7. The lamp test bank lights when placed from point L to point N but does not light when placed from point M to point P.
   It should be concluded that

   A. both fuses x and y are bad
   B. either fuse x or fuse y is bad or both are bad
   C. both fuses x and y are good
   D. these tests do not indicate the condition of any fuse

8. The lamp test bank is placed from point L to point N, then from N to point Q, and finally from point L to point Q. In each case, both lamps light to full brightness.
   It should be concluded that points L, N, and Q have

   A. three-phase, 120 volts, AC, line-to-line
   B. plus and minus 120 volts, DC
   C. three-phase, 208 volts, AC
   D. plus and minus 240 volts, DC

9. An automatic device used for regulating air temperature is a(n)

   A. rheostat   B. aquastat   C. thermostat   D. duostat

10. Assume that you have just completed a certain maintenance job which you feel is satisfactory, but your foreman asks you to make certain changes.
    The BEST procedure for you to follow is to

    A. request the foreman to assign this work to someone else
    B. have another maintainer verify that the job was done properly
    C. ask the foreman the reasons for the changes
    D. complain to the foreman's superior of this waste of time

11. The PROPER set of tools and equipment to be used to clean and adjust the ignition points of an automobile consists of a

    A. screwdriver, feeler gauge, and point file
    B. wrench, micrometer, and sandpaper
    C. scraper, micrometer, and emery cloth
    D. V-block, pliers, and sandpaper

12. The voltage developed in each cell of an automobile battery is _____ volts.

    A. 2   B. 4   C. 6   D. 12

13. The one of the following tools that is NOT used to clear plumbing stoppages is a

    A. force-cup   B. drain auger
    C. snake   D. pick-out iron

14. Eyebolts are generally fastened to the shells of machinery in order to

    A. act as a leveling device
    B. facilitate lifting
    C. permit easy tagging of the equipment
    D. reinforce the machine shells

15. When grinding a weld smooth, it is MOST important to avoid

    A. grinding too slowly
    B. overheating the surrounding metal
    C. grinding away too much of the weld
    D. grinding after the weld has cooled off

16. A cold chisel whose head has become *mushroomed* should NOT be used because

    A. it is impossible to hit the head squarely
    B. the chisel will not cut accurately
    C. chips might fly from the head
    D. the chisel has lost its *temper*

17. The type of screwdriver specially made to be used in tight spots is the

    A. Phillips   B. offset
    C. square shank   D. truss

18. An indication that a fluorescent lamp in a fixture should be replaced is

    A. humming in the fixture
    B. the ends of the lamp remain black when the lamp is lit
    C. poor or slow starting
    D. the lamp does not shut off each time the OFF button is pressed

19. Asbestos is used as a covering on electrical wires to provide protection from

    A. high voltage   B. high temperatures
    C. water damage   D. electrolysis

20. Many electric power tools, such as drills, have a third conductor in the line cord which should be connected to a grounded part of the power receptacle.
    The reason for this is to

    A. have a spare wire in case one power wire should break
    B. strengthen the power lead so that it cannot be easily damaged
    C. protect the user of the tool from electrical shocks
    D. allow use of the tool for extended periods of time without overheating

21. Employees are responsible for the good care, proper maintenance, and serviceable condition of the property issued or assigned for their use.
    As used above, *serviceable condition* means the property is in a state where it is

    A. capable of being repaired   B. easily handled
    C. fit for use   D. least expensive

22. A brush that has been used in shellac should be cleaned by washing it in

    A. water   B. linseed oil
    C. lacquer thinner D. alcohol

23. Excessive moisture on a surface being painted would MOST likely result in

    A. alligatoring   B. blistering
    C. cracking   D. sagging

24. In order to reverse the direction of rotation of a series motor, the

    A. connections to the armature should be reversed
    B. connections to both the armature and the series field should be reversed
    C. connections of the motor to the power lines should be reversed
    D. series field should be placed in shunt with the armature

25. A megger is an instrument used to measure

    A. capacitance   B. insulation resistance
    C. power   D. illumination levels

26. The first aid treatment for chemical burns on the skin is

    A. treatment with ointment and then bandaging
    B. washing with large quantities of water and then treating as heat burns
    C. treatment with a neutralizing agent and no bandaging
    D. application of sodium bicarbonate and then bandaging

27. The chemical MOST frequently used to clean drains clogged with grease is 27.____

    A. muriatic acid B. soda ash
    C. ammonia D. caustic soda

28. When tapping a blind hole in a steel plate, the FIRST type of tap to use is a _____ tap. 28.____

    A. plug B. taper C. lead D. bottoming

29. A common handshaving tool used in woodwork is a(n) 29.____

    A. trammel B. router C. auger D. plane

30. *Dressing* a grinding wheel refers to 30.____

    A. making the wheel thinner
    B. replacing with a new wheel
    C. repairing a crack in the wheel
    D. making the wheel round

31. The maintainer who is MOST valuable is the one who 31.____

    A. offers to do the heavy lifting
    B. asks many questions about the work
    C. listens to instructions and carries them out
    D. makes many suggestions on work procedures

32. Of the following, turpentine is used for thinning 32.____

    A. latex paint B. red lead paint
    C. calcimine D. shellac

33. Of the following, the hacksaw blade BEST suited for cutting thin-walled tubing is one which has _____ teeth/inch. 33.____

    A. 14 B. 18 C. 24 D. 32

34. Because of its weather-resistant properties, a varnish commonly used on exterior surfaces is _____ varnish. 34.____

    A. spar B. flat C. rubbing D. hard oil

35. A trip spring or spring cylinder on a snow plow assembly is a device that 35.____

    A. absorbs the shock of impact when the plow strikes an obstacle in the road
    B. provides for snap-action in the lowering of the plow blade
    C. allows for quick removal or attachment of the snow plow supporting frame
    D. detaches the plow blade and lets it hang free when the plow blade is dragged backwards

36. The term *preventative maintenance* is used to identify a plan whereby 36.____

    A. equipment is serviced according to a regular schedule
    B. equipment is serviced as soon as it fails
    C. equipment is replaced as soon as it becomes obsolete
    D. all equipment is replaced periodically

37. The ratio of air to gasoline in an automobile engine is controlled by the

    A. gas filter B. fuel pump
    C. carburetor D. intake manifold

38. *Energizer* is another name given to the

    A. automobile battery B. fluorescent fixture ballast
    C. battery charger D. generator shunt field

39. Wearshoes may be found on

    A. circuit breakers B. automobile brake systems
    C. snow plows D. door sills

40. When moving heavy equipment by means of pipe rollers, it is MOST important to

    A. use solid steel rollers
    B. use rollers with different diameters
    C. see that the trailing roller does not slip out from under the equipment
    D. use more than three rollers at all times

41. The one of the following storage areas that is BEST for the storage of paint is one which is

    A. unheated and not ventilated
    B. cool and ventilated
    C. sunny and ventilated
    D. warm and not ventilated

42. The leverage that can be obtained with a wrench is determined mainly by the

    A. material of which the wrench is made
    B. gripping surface of the jaw
    C. length of the handle
    D. thickness of the wrench

43. A star drill is used to bore holes in

    A. steel B. concrete C. wood D. sheet metal

44. The one of the following actions of a maintainer that is MOST likely to contribute to a good working relationship between him and his assistant is for him to

    A. observe the same rules of conduct that he expects his assistant to observe
    B. freely give advice on his assistant's personal problems
    C. always be frank and outspoken to his assistant in pointing out his faults
    D. expect his assistant to perform with equal efficiency on any job assigned

45. Three common types of windows are

    A. batten, casement, and awning
    B. batten, casement, and double-hung
    C. batten, double-hung, and awning
    D. casement, double-hung, and awning

46. A staircase has twelve risers, each 6 3/4" high. The TOTAL rise of the staircase is

    A. 6'2 1/4"   B. 6'9"   C. 7'0"   D. 7'3 3/4"

47. A twenty-foot straight ladder placed at an angle against a wall should be at a distance from the wall equal to _____ feet.

    A. 3   B. 5   C. 7   D. 9

48. Reflective sheeting traffic signs that have become dirty should be wiped with kerosene or gasoline FOLLOWED by a

    A. wiping with a soft cloth soaked in thin oil
    B. hand rub with very fine sandpaper
    C. wash with detergent and a rinse with water
    D. coating of shellac applied with a brush

49. A temporary wooden fence carrying red flags and built around an opening in a pavement to warn oncoming traffic is known as a

    A. batter board   B. bulkhead
    C. bollard   D. barricade

50. *Four-ply belted* is used to describe the construction of

    A. belt-drive pulleys
    B. auto tires
    C. electrical wiring insulation
    D. seat belts

KEY (CORRECT ANSWERS)

1. A	11. A	21. C	31. C	41. B
2. D	12. A	22. D	32. B	42. C
3. D	13. D	23. B	33. D	43. B
4. B	14. B	24. A	34. A	44. A
5. D	15. C	25. B	35. A	45. D
6. C	16. C	26. B	36. A	46. B
7. B	17. B	27. D	37. C	47. B
8. C	18. B	28. B	38. A	48. C
9. C	19. B	29. D	39. C	49. D
10. C	20. C	30. D	40. C	50. B

TEST 2

DIRECTIONS: Each question or incomplete statement is followed by several suggested answers or completions. Select the one that BEST answers the question or completes the statement. *PRINT THE LETTER OF THE CORRECT ANSWER IN THE SPACE AT THE RIGHT.*

1. An oil bath filter is MOST often used on a(n)
   - A. air compressor
   - B. auto engine
   - C. electric generator
   - D. steam boiler

2. A 3-ohm resistor placed across a 12-volt battery will dissipate _____ watts.
   - A. 3
   - B. 4
   - C. 12
   - D. 48

3. Instead of using fuses, modern electric wiring uses
   - A. quick switches
   - B. circuit breakers
   - C. fusible links
   - D. lag blocks

4. The MOST common combination of gases used for welding is
   - A. carbon dioxide and acetylene
   - B. nitrogen and hydrogen
   - C. oxygen and acetylene
   - D. oxygen and hydrogen

5. If a wheel has turned through an angle of 180, then it has made _____ revolution(s).
   - A. 1/4
   - B. 1/2
   - C. 1/8
   - D. 18

6. Sewer gas is prevented from backing up through a plumbing fixture by a
   - A. water trap
   - B. return elbow
   - C. check valve
   - D. float valve

7. Putty that is too stiff is made workable by adding
   - A. gasoline
   - B. linseed oil
   - C. water
   - D. lacquer thinner

8. A vertical wood member in the wall of a wood frame house is known as a
   - A. A stringer
   - B. ridge member
   - C. stud
   - D. header

9. A 10-to-1 step-down transformer has an input of 1 ampere at 120 volts AC. If the losses are negligible, the output of the transformer is _____ volts.
   - A. 1 ampere at 12
   - B. .1 ampere at 1200
   - C. 10 amperes at 12
   - D. 10 amperes at 120

10. An oscilloscope is an instrument used in
    - A. measuring noise levels
    - B. displaying waveforms of electrical signals
    - C. indicating the concentrations of pollutants in air
    - D. photographing high-speed events

11. Assume that a brake pedal of a truck goes to the floorboard when depressed. The one of the following that could cause this condition is

    A. a leak in the hydraulic lines
    B. a clogged hydraulic line
    C. scored drums
    D. glazed linings

11.____

12. The universal joints of an automobile are located on the

    A. suspension springs   B. steering linkages
    C. wheel cylinders   D. drive shaft

12.____

13. The MAIN purpose of a flexible coupling is to connect two shafts which are

    A. of different diameters   B. of different shapes
    C. not in exact alignment   D. of different material

13.____

14. When using a standard measuring micrometer, starting with a zero reading, one complete counterclockwise revolution of the sleeve will give a reading of _____ inch.

    A. .001   B. .010   C. .025   D. .250

14.____

15. If a nut is to be tightened to an exact specified value of inch-lbs., the wrench to use is a _____ wrench.

    A. spanner   B. box   C. lock-jaw   D. torque

15.____

16. Common permanent type anti-freezes for automobile cooling systems are MAINLY

    A. alcohol   B. methanol
    C. ethylene glycol   D. trychloroethylene

16.____

17. Plexiglas is also called

    A. mylar   B. lucite   C. isinglass   D. PVC

17.____

18. Long, curved lines are BEST cut in 1/4" plexiglas with a _____ saw.

    A. rip   B. jig   C. keyhole   D. coping

18.____

19. The specific gravity of storage battery cells can be measured with a(n)

    A. odometer   B. hydrometer C. ammeter   D. dwell meter

19.____

20. A nail set is a tool used for

    A. straightening bent nails
    B. measuring nail sizes
    C. cutting nails to specified size
    D. driving a nail head into wood

20.____

21. To cut a number of 2" x 4" lengths of wood accurately at an angle of 45°, it is BEST to use a

    A. protractor B. mitre-box   C. triangle   D. square

21.____

22. The type of fastener MOST commonly used when bolting to concrete uses a(n)

    A. expansion shield   B. U-bolt
    C. toggle bolt   D. turnbuckle

23. When an automobile engine does not start on a damp day, the trouble is MOST likely in the _____ system.

    A. ignition   B. cooling   C. fuel   D. lubricating

24. The battery of an automobile is prevented from discharging back through the alternator by the blocking action of the

    A. commutator   B. diodes   C. brushes   D. slip rings

25. The master cylinder in an automobile is actuated by the

    A. steering column   B. brake pedal
    C. clutch plate   D. cam shaft

26. The FINEST sandpaper from among the following is No.

    A. 3   B. 1   C. 2/0   D. 6/0

27. A screw whose head is buried below the surface of the wood that it is screwed into is said to be

    A. countersunk   B. scalloped
    C. expanded   D. flushed

28. The one of the following devices which is used to measure angles is the

    A. caliper   B. protractor
    C. marking gauge   D. divider

29. Before a new oil stone is used, it should be

    A. heated   B. soaked in oil
    C. coated with shellac   D. washed with soapy water

30. Dies are used for

    A. threading the outside ends of metal pipes
    B. making sweated joints on lead pipes
    C. cutting nipples to exact lengths
    D. caulking cast-iron pipe joints

31. The energy stored by a storage battery is commonly given in

    A. volts   B. amperes
    C. ampere-hours   D. kilowatts

32. *Vapor lock* occurs in automobile

    A. gas tanks   B. crankcases
    C. transmissions   D. carburetors

33. A woodworking tool used to bore odd-size holes for which there is no standard auger bit is a(n)

   A. single twist auger
   B. double twist auger
   C. expansive bit
   D. straight fluted drill

34. Soap is sometimes applied to wood screws in order to

   A. prevent rust
   B. make a tight fit
   C. make insertion easier
   D. prevent wood splitting

35. On a long run of copper tubing, the tubing is often bent in the shape of a horseshoe rather than being run in a straight line.
   The MAIN reason for this is to

   A. allow an excess that could be used in future repairs
   B. make it easier to install the tubing
   C. permit the tubing to expand and contract with changes in temperature
   D. eliminate the need for accurate measurements in cutting the tubing

36. Loss of seal water in a house water trap is prevented by the use of a

   A. drainage tee   B. faucet   C. hose bibb   D. vent

37. BX is a designation for a type of

   A. flexible armored electric cable
   B. flexible gas line
   C. rigid conduit
   D. electrical insulation

38. *WYE-WYE* and *DELTA-WYE* are two

   A. types of DC motor windings
   B. arrangements of 3-phase transformer connections
   C. types of electrical splices
   D. shapes of commutator bars

39. Green lumber should NOT be used in the building of scaffolding because it

   A. will not hold nails well
   B. easily splits when nailed
   C. may warp on drying
   D. is too expensive

40. *Scotchlite* ready-made traffic sign faces with heat-activated adhesive backings are applied to backing blanks by use of a

   A. temperature-controlled oven
   B. vacuum applicator
   C. hot water bath
   D. heated roller assembly

41. *Scotchcal* is a(n)

   A. reflective sheeting
   B. epoxy protective paint
   C. fluorescent film
   D. high temperature lubricant

42. Wooden ladders should NOT be painted because the paint

    A. is inflammable
    B. may cover defects in the wood
    C. makes the rungs slippery
    D. may deteriorate the wood

43. To prevent ladders from slipping, the bottoms of the ladder side rails are OFTEN fitted with

    A. automatic locks   B. ladder shoes
    C. ladder hooks   D. stirrups

44. A bowline is

    A. the sag that a scaffold develops when men get on it
    B. a knot with a loop that does not run
    C. a temporary telephone wire strung during emergencies
    D. the reference line established in ditch excavations

45. A method sometimes used to prevent a pipe from buckling during a bending operation is to

    A. bend the pipe very quickly
    B. keep the seam of the pipe on the outside of the bend
    C. nick the pipe at the center of the bend
    D. pack the inside of the pipe with sand

46. A rectifier changes

    A. DC to AC
    B. AC to DC
    C. single-phase power to three-phase power
    D. battery power to three-phase power

47. Continuity in a de-energized electrical circuit may be checked with a(n)

    A. voltmeter   B. ohmmeter   C. neon tester   D. rheostat

48. Of the following crankcase oils, the one that should be used in sub-zero weather is SAE

    A. 10W   B. 20W   C. 20   D. 30

49. Caster in an automobile is an adjustment in the

    A. ignition system   B. drive-shaft
    C. rear differential   D. front suspension

50. If the spark plugs in an engine run too hot, the result is MOST likely that

    A. oil and carbon compounds will accumulate on the insulators
    B. the electrodes will wear rapidly
    C. the timing will be retarded
    D. the ignition coil may become damaged

KEY (CORRECT ANSWERS)

1. B	11. A	21. B	31. C	41. C
2. B	12. D	22. A	32. D	42. B
3. B	13. C	23. A	33. C	43. B
4. C	14. C	24. B	34. C	44. B
5. B	15. D	25. B	35. C	45. D
6. A	16. C	26. D	36. D	46. B
7. B	17. B	27. A	37. A	47. B
8. C	18. B	28. B	38. B	48. A
9. C	19. B	29. B	39. C	49. D
10. B	20. D	30. A	40. B	50. B

EXAMINATION SECTION
TEST 1

DIRECTIONS: Each question or incomplete statement is followed by several suggested answers or completions. Select the one that BEST answers the question or completes the statement. *PRINT THE LETTER OF THE CORRECT ANSWER IN THE SPACE AT THE RIGHT.*

1. When assembling a piece of equipment which has been disassembled, a part which can *usually* be re-used is a

    A. gasket
    B. flat washer
    C. cotter pin
    D. lock washer

2. An offset screwdriver is MOST useful for turning a wood screw when

    A. a strong force needs to be applied
    B. the screw head is marred
    C. space is limited
    D. speed is desired

3. The plug of a portable tool should be removed from a receptacle by grasping the plug, and NOT by pulling on the cord, because

    A. the plug is easier to grip than the cord
    B. pulling on the cord may allow the plug to fall on the floor and break
    C. the plug is generally better insulated than the cord
    D. pulling on the cord may break the wires off the plug

4. Of the following orders for tools or materials used in the building trades, the one which is INCOMPLETE is

    A. 1 paintbrush, flat, 2 in. wide
    B. 1 drill, twist, straight shank, high speed, 3/8 in.
    C. 1 snake, steel, 3/4 in. wide by 1/8 in. thick
    D. 1 keg of nails, 10 penny, common wire, galvanized

5. The tool that is *generally* used to slightly elongate a round hole in strap-iron is a

    A. rat-tail file
    B. reamer
    C. drill
    D. rasp

6. If a fellow worker has stopped breathing after an electric shock, the BEST first-aid treatment is

    A. artificial respiration
    B. to massage his chest
    C. an application of cold compresses
    D. a hot drink

7. Lumber used in certain types of outdoor construction work is treated with creosote before being used. The creosote serves to

    A. decrease the rusting of the nails used for fastening
    B. prevent the lumber from checking or peeling

43

C. act as a good undercoat for paint
D. prevent the lumber from rotting

8. Drilling must be done with special care when using any one of the very small sizes of twist drills because the

   A. drill is apt to break
   B. drill is apt to overheat
   C. cut material will clog the drill
   D. drill speed may be too fast

9. The BEST way to locate a point on the floor directly below a given point on the ceiling is by using a

   A. plumber's snake   B. plumb bob
   C. flashlight   D. chalk line

10. When the term "10-24" is used to specify a machine screw, the number 24 refers to the

    A. number of screws per pound
    B. diameter of the screw
    C. length of the screw
    D. number of threads per inch

11. In the run of piping, the dimension marked "X" is
    A. 19"
    B. 11"
    C. 9"
    D. 5"

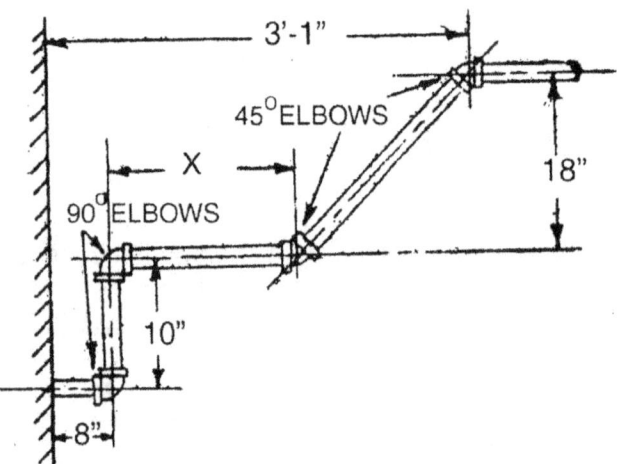

12. The *approximate* dimensions of a common brick are as shown. The volume of the brick (in cubic feet) is
    A. 64
    B. 5 1/3
    C. 4/9
    D. 1/27

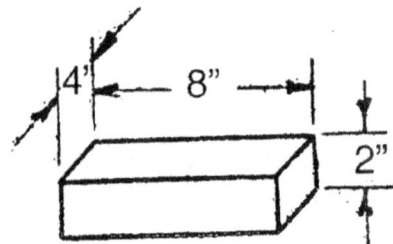

13. If the shaded portion is cut from the plate shown, the area (in square inches) of the remaining portion is
    A. 26
    B. 29
    C. 32
    D. 58

14. A nut is shown with a wrench placed on it in positions 1 and 2. The numbered arrows show the directions of forces applied to the wrench to turn it. In order to tighten the nut, the CORRECT combination of wrench position and direction of applied force is
    A. 1-3
    B. 1-4
    C. 2-5
    D. 2-6

15. Shown is an open-top round tin container. In order to make the container so that the metal used for the bottom area (πR^2) is equal to the metal used for the cylindrical side area ($2 \pi Rh$), the radius $\underline{R}$ must be equal to
    A. 1/2"
    B. 1"
    C. 2"
    D. 4"

16. Tools used in maintenance work should ALWAYS be kept in good condition because

    A. a good job can never be done without perfect tools
    B. tools that are in good condition require no care
    C. defective tools may cause accidents or damage
    D. good tools are less easily lost

17. If you are assigned by your foreman to a job which you do NOT understand, you should

    A. try to do the job because you learn from experience
    B. explain and request further instructions from your foreman
    C. do the job to the best of your ability as that is all that can be expected
    D. ask a more experienced helper how to proceed with the job

18. When wooden forms used in concrete work are taken down, the nails in the lumber which is saved for future use are removed rather than bent over and clinched. The purpose of this procedure is to

A. prevent the old nails from being unbent and used again
B. prevent the possible staining of the concrete by contact with rusty nails
C. avoid damage to the saw if the lumber is cut
D. permit future use of the same nail holes

19. Twist drills ranging in size from 5/16" to 1/2" and having 1/4" shanks are available for use in electric drills. These drills are designed in this manner so that they may be used

    A. in 1/4" electric drills for high speed drilling of steel
    B. in 1/4" electric drills for drilling wood
    C. when it is important that, if the twist drill breaks, it does not do so in the hole being drilled
    D. in 1/2" electric drills in order to increase the peripheral speed of the twist drill

19.____

20. The wrench is shown in position to unloosen a tight nut. If the hand is placed on the wrench at A, the force necessary to start the nut as compared to the force necessary if the hand were placed at B would be
    A. 150%
    B. 110%
    C. 85%
    D. 70%

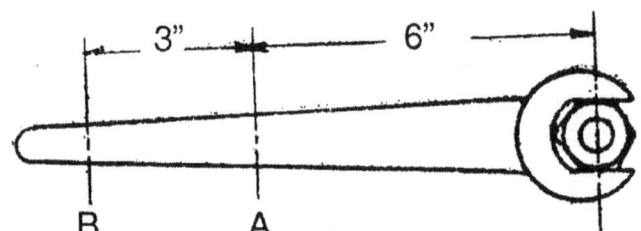

20.____

21. With the valve closed, each of the two identical tanks holds water in the amount shown. If the valve is opened, the amount of water (in gallons) in tanks X and Y after flow has stopped will be, respectively,
    A. 6000-5000
    B. 5500-5500
    C. 5000-6000
    D. 3500-7500

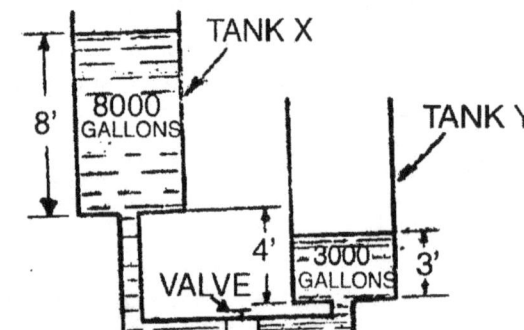

21.____

22. If the windlass shown is turned clockwise by means of the crank and handle at a rate of 35 revolutions per minute, the weight will rise at a rate of _____ ft. per minute.
    A. 65
    B. 110
    C. 235
    D. 480

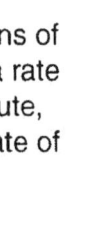
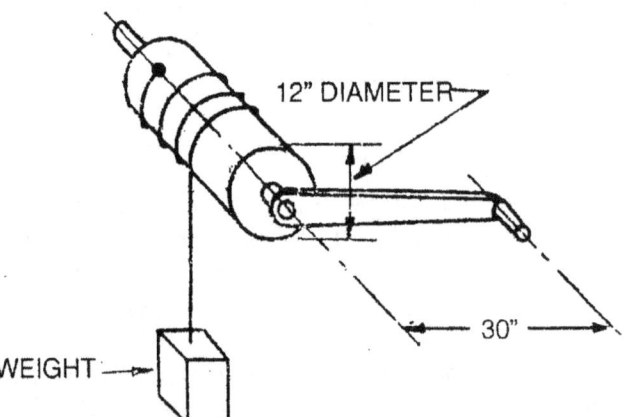

22.____

23. In order to have the two stringlines perpendicular to each other, the distance "X" on the tape must be _____ ft.
    A. 21
    B. 16
    C. 15
    D. 14

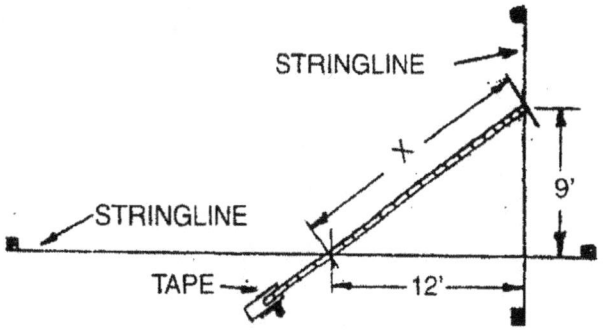

24. The dimension "X" on the plate is
    A. 1 7/8"
    B. 2 1/8"
    C. 2 1/4"
    D. 2 3/8"

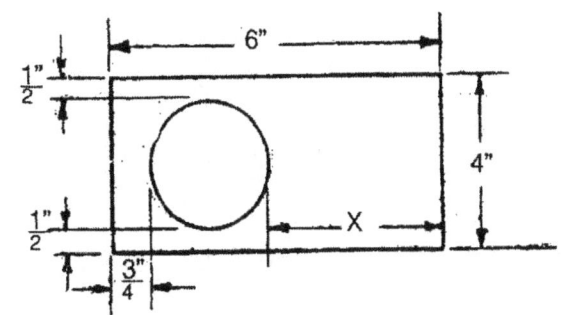

QUESTIONS 25-30.

Questions 25-30 inclusive in Column I are structural materials each of which would be ordered by using one of the quantity-terms listed in Column II. For each material in Column I, select the appropriate quantity-term from Column II. PRINT on your answer sheet, in the correspondingly numbered item space, the letter given beside your selected quantity-term.

Column I (structural materials)	Column II (quantity-term)
25. sandpaper	A. cartons
	B. feet
26. paint	C. pounds
	D. bags
27. cinders	E. gallons
	H. rolls
28. sash cord	J. square feet
	K. cubic yards
29. cement	L. sheets
30. nails	

KEY (CORRECT ANSWERS)

1.	B	16.	C
2.	C	17.	B
3.	D	18.	C
4.	C	19.	B
5.	A	20.	A
6.	A	21.	D
7.	D	22.	B
8.	A	23.	C
9.	B	24.	C
10.	D	25.	L
11.	B	26.	E
12.	D	27.	K
13.	C	28.	B
14.	D	29.	D
15.	D	30.	C

TEST 2

DIRECTIONS: Each question or incomplete statement is followed by several suggested answers or completions. Select the one that BEST answers the question or completes the Statement. *PRINT THE LETTER OF THE CORRECT ANSWER IN THE SPACE AT THE RIGHT.*

QUESTIONS 1-10.

Questions 1-10 inclusive in Column I are materials each of which is commonly identified for size by one of the terms listed in Column II. For each material in Column I, select the appropriate size-term from Column II. Print in the correspondingly numbered item space the letter given beside your selected size-term.

Column I (materials)		Column II (size terms)	
1.	strap iron	A.	20 gauge
2.	manila rope	B.	3/4"
3.	steel wool	C.	1/2" x 6"
4.	carriage bolts	D.	8" x 8" x 16"
5.	steel sheets	E.	1/8" x 2 1/2"
6.	plywood panels	H.	#8 x 3/4"
7.	copper tacks	J.	No. 6
8.	wood screws	K.	3/4" x 1/2"
9.	cement blocks	L.	4' x 4' x 3/4"
10.	pipe reducer	M.	#00

1.____
2.____
3.____
4.____
5.____
6.____
7.____
8.____
9.____
10.____

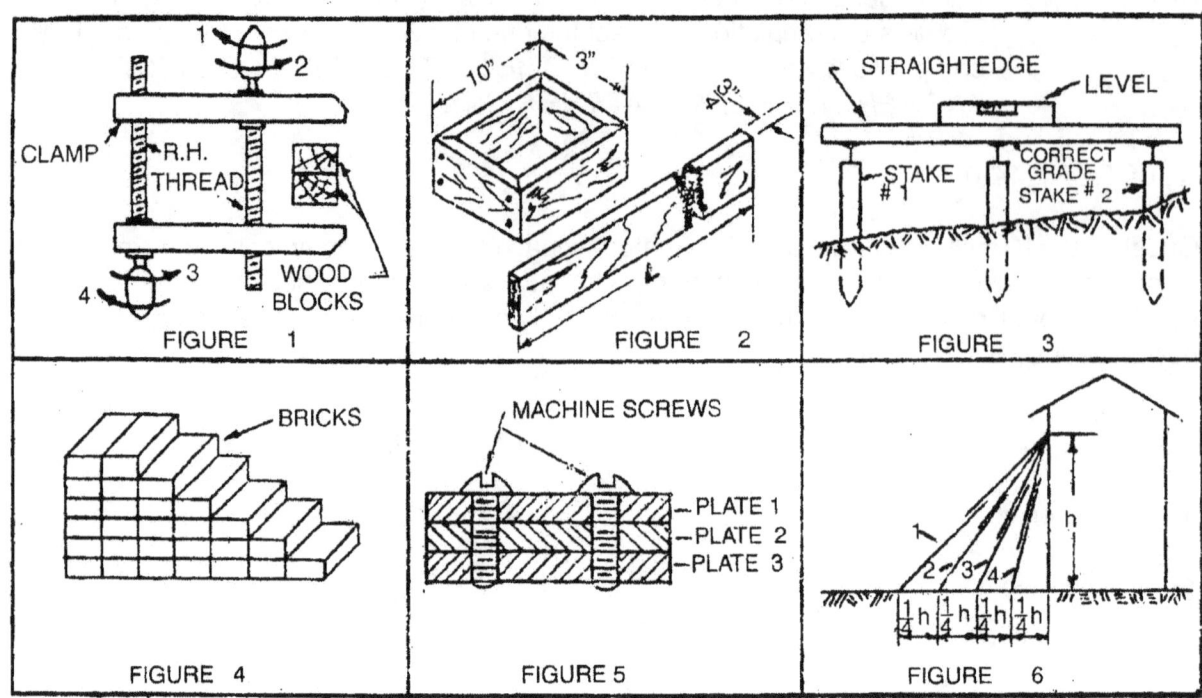

QUESTIONS 11-16.

Questions 11-16 inclusive refer to the figures above.

11. In Figure 1, in order to press together the two wood blocks, the handles of the clamp should be turned in the directions

    A. 1-3   B. 1-4   C. 2-3   D. 2-4

12. In order to make the form shown in Figure 2 from the board also shown, the length "L" of the board (making allowance for 1/8" saw-cuts) should NOT be LESS than

    A. 32 1/2"   B. 34 1/2"   C. 35 1/2"   D. 38 1/2"

13. In Figure 3, in order to obtain the correct grade at stakes #1 and #2, it will be necessary to LOWER the nail in stake

    A. #1
    B. #2
    C. #1 and RAISE the nail in stake #2
    D. #2 and RAISE the nail in stake #1

14. In Figure 4, in order to rearrange the bricks shown into the LEAST number of equal piles, the number of bricks required to be moved is

    A. 11   B. 10   C. 9   D. 8

15. To fasten the three metal plates in Figure 5 together with machine screws as shown, the *proper* method is to tap

    A. all three plates   B. plate 3 *only*
    C. plates 2 and 3 *only*   D. plates 1 and 3 *only*

3 (#2)

16. In Figure 6, the extension ladder is shown placed in four different positions against the side of a house. The CORRECT position is

    A. 1 B. 2 C. 3 D. 4

16.____

17. The width (in inches) of each of the identical slots in the plate is
    A. 1/4
    B. 3/16
    C. 1/8
    D. 1/16

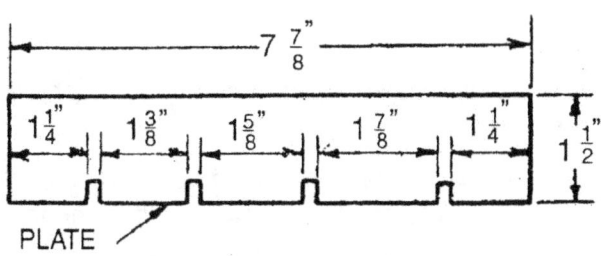

17.____

18. The number of feet of wire fencing needed to enclose the area shown is
    A. 100
    B. 140
    C. 150
    D. 170

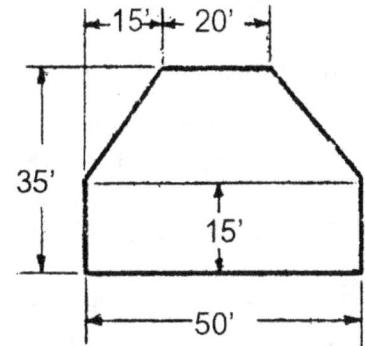

18.____

19. To bring the level of the water in the two open-top tanks down to a height of 6 inches, the quantity of water to be removed by opening the valve is _____ gallons.
    A. 10 1/2
    B. 9
    C. 7 1/2
    D. 6

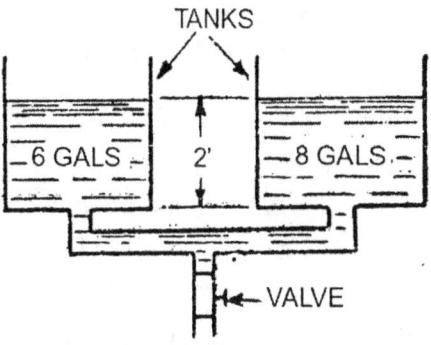

19.____

20. If concrete weighs 150 lbs. per cubic foot, the weight of the concrete manhole shown (open top and bottom) is
    A. between 1/2 ton and 1 ton
    B. exactly 1 ton
    C. between 1 ton and 1 1/2 tons
    D. exactly 2 tons

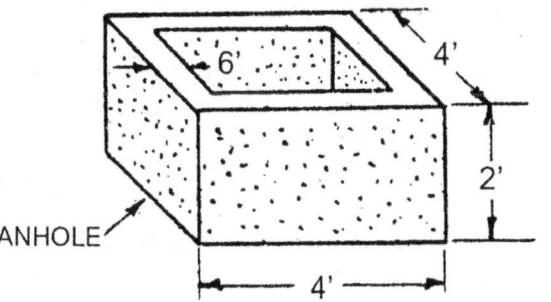

20.____

21. The MAXIMUM number of gaskets shown which can be cut from the gasket material as shown is
    A. 19
    B. 60
    C. 135
    D. 270

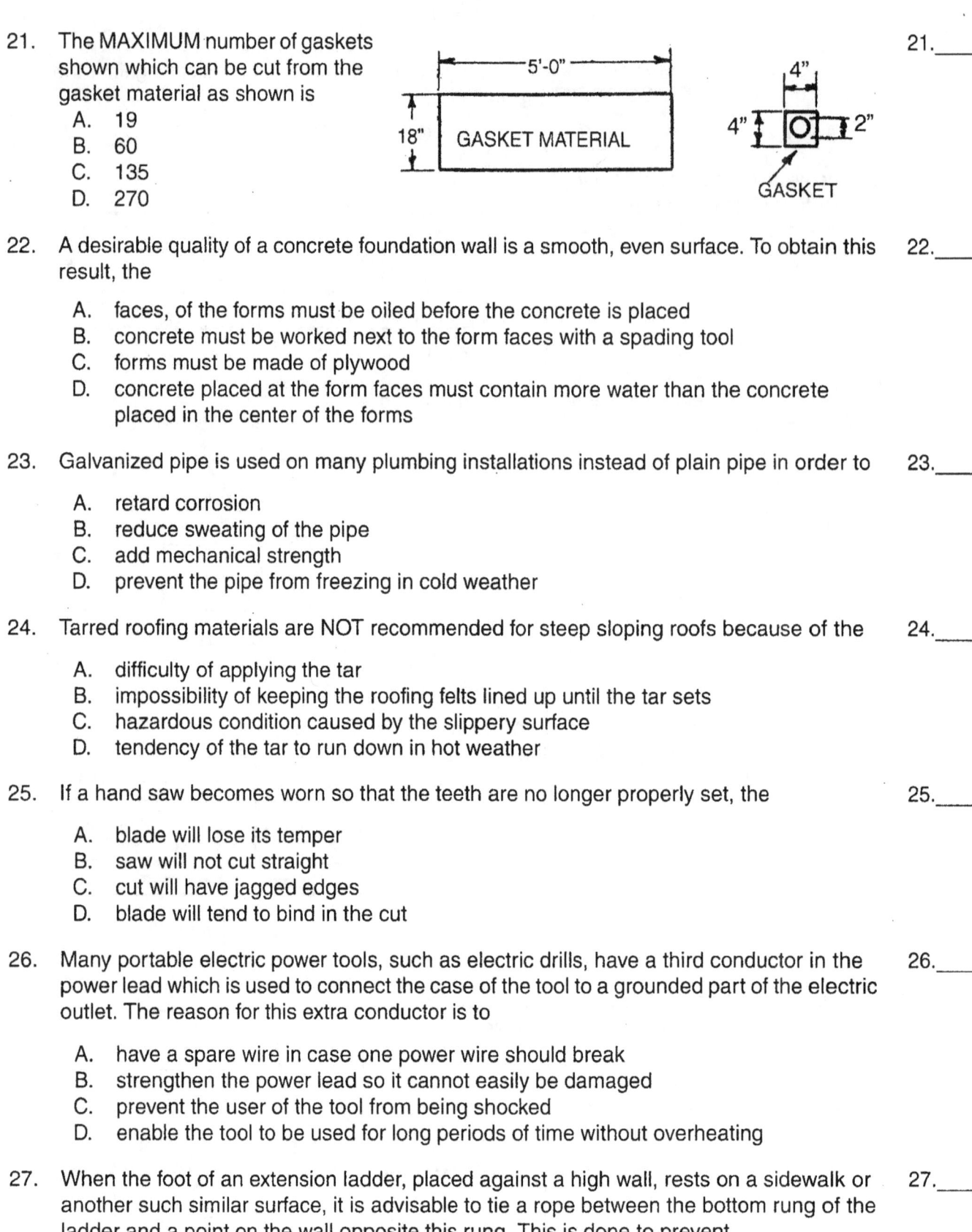

22. A desirable quality of a concrete foundation wall is a smooth, even surface. To obtain this result, the
    A. faces, of the forms must be oiled before the concrete is placed
    B. concrete must be worked next to the form faces with a spading tool
    C. forms must be made of plywood
    D. concrete placed at the form faces must contain more water than the concrete placed in the center of the forms

23. Galvanized pipe is used on many plumbing installations instead of plain pipe in order to
    A. retard corrosion
    B. reduce sweating of the pipe
    C. add mechanical strength
    D. prevent the pipe from freezing in cold weather

24. Tarred roofing materials are NOT recommended for steep sloping roofs because of the
    A. difficulty of applying the tar
    B. impossibility of keeping the roofing felts lined up until the tar sets
    C. hazardous condition caused by the slippery surface
    D. tendency of the tar to run down in hot weather

25. If a hand saw becomes worn so that the teeth are no longer properly set, the
    A. blade will lose its temper
    B. saw will not cut straight
    C. cut will have jagged edges
    D. blade will tend to bind in the cut

26. Many portable electric power tools, such as electric drills, have a third conductor in the power lead which is used to connect the case of the tool to a grounded part of the electric outlet. The reason for this extra conductor is to
    A. have a spare wire in case one power wire should break
    B. strengthen the power lead so it cannot easily be damaged
    C. prevent the user of the tool from being shocked
    D. enable the tool to be used for long periods of time without overheating

27. When the foot of an extension ladder, placed against a high wall, rests on a sidewalk or another such similar surface, it is advisable to tie a rope between the bottom rung of the ladder and a point on the wall opposite this rung. This is done to prevent
    A. people from walking under the ladder
    B. another worker from removing the ladder

C. the ladder from vibrating when ascending or descending
D. the foot of the ladder from slipping

28. If you were unable to tighten a nut by means of a ratchet wrench because, although the nut turned on with the forward movement of the wrench, it turned off with the backward movement, you should

   A. make the nut hand-tight before using the wrench
   B. reverse the ratchet action
   C. put a few drops of oil on the wrench
   D. use a different socket in the handle

28._____

29. If you were installing a long wood screw and found you were unable to drive this screw more than three-quarters of its length by the use of a properly-fitting straight-handled screwdriver, the PROPER subsequent action would be for you to

   A. take out the screw and put soap on it
   B. change to the use of a screwdriver-bit and brace
   C. take out the screw and drill a deeper hole before re-driving
   D. use a pair of pliers on the blade of the screwdriver

29._____

30. Good practice requires that the end of a pipe to be installed in a plumbing system be reamed to remove the inside burr after it has been cut to length to

   A. restore the original inside diameter of the pipe at the end
   B. remove loose rust
   C. make the threading of the pipe easier
   D. finish the pipe accurately to length

30._____

KEY (CORRECT ANSWERS)

1.	E	16.	D
2.	B	17.	C
3.	M	18.	C
4.	C	19.	A
5.	A	20.	C
6.	L	21.	B
7.	J	22.	B
8.	H	23.	A
9.	D	24.	D
10.	K	25.	D
11.	A	26.	C
12.	B	27.	D
13.	C	28.	A
14.	B	29.	A/C
15.	B	30.	A

TEST 3

DIRECTIONS: Each question or incomplete statement is followed by several suggested answers or completions. Select the one that BEST answers the question or completes the statement. *PRINT THE LETTER OF THE CORRECT ANSWER IN THE SPACE AT THE RIGHT.*

1. When laying tongue and groove flooring, each piece is laid with the tongue to the front and the groove fitted to the tongue of the previously laid piece. In order to make this a tight fit before nailing into place, it is GOOD practice when laying each piece to 1.____

    A. temporarily toe-nail through its tongue to draw it up tight
    B. fit a small piece of scrap flooring to it and strike the scrap piece
    C. strike it only on the middle of the tongue
    D. pull it into place using a chisel as a pry bar

2. In construction work, *almost all* accidents can be blamed on the 2.____

    A. failure of an individual to give close attention to the job assigned to him
    B. use of improper tools
    C. lack of cooperation among the men in a gang
    D. fact that an incompetent man was placed in a key position

3. If it is necessary for you to do some work with your hands under a piece of heavy equipment, while a fellow worker lifts up and holds one end of it by means of a pinch bar, one IMPORTANT precaution you should take is to 3.____

    A. wear gloves
    B. watch the bar to be ready if it slips
    C. insert a temporary block to support the piece
    D. work as fast as possible

4. Protective goggles should NOT be worn when 4.____

    A. standing on a ladder drilling a steel beam
    B. descending a ladder after completing a job
    C. chipping concrete near a third rail
    D. sharpening a cold chisel on a grinding stone

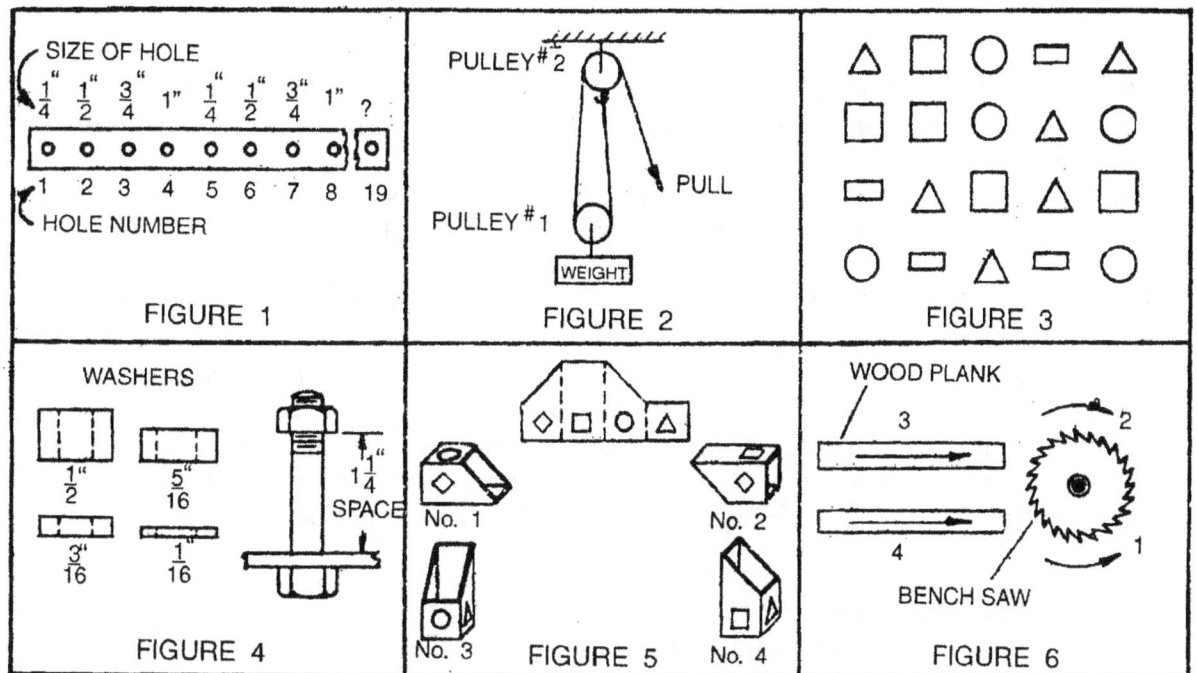

QUESTIONS 5-10.

Questions 5-10 inclusive refer to the figures above.

5. If the holes shown in Figure 1 continue in the same pattern along the entire strip, the 19th hole would be

   A. 1/4"   B. 1/2"   C. 3/4"   D. 1"

   5.____

6. In Figure 2, the block and tackle shown has two pulleys of equal diameter. While the weight is being raised, pulley #2 will rotate at _____ the speed of pulley #1.

   A. twice   B. one time   C. one-half   D. one-third

   6.____

7. Figure 3 shows four basic shapes. The shapes appearing the MOST number of times is

   A. A   B. B   C. C   D. D

   7.____

8. In figure 4, using only the sizes of washers shown, the LEAST number of washers needed to *exactly* fill the 1 1/4" space is

   A. 7   B. 6   C. 4   D. 2

   8.____

9. The flat cut sheet in Figure 5, with cut-outs as shown, can be bent along the dotted lines to make one of the shapes shown. The resulting shape is No.

   A. 1   B. 2   C. 3   D. 4

   9.____

10. Figure 6 shows a bench saw with directions of rotation 1 and 2, and a plank ready for cutting in positions 3 and 4. The *proper* combination of rotation and position is

    A. 1 and 3   B. 1 and 4   C. 2 and 3   D. 2 and 4

    10.____

11. In preparing to raise a steel beam to position during steel erection, the man placing the slings puts only one sling near the center of the beam rather than a sling at each end. This procedure is

    A. *poor* because of the possibility of the beam slipping through the one sling
    B. *good* because it allows the beam to be tilted at the ends for necessary maneuvering
    C. *poor* because the safeguards against sling breakage is cut in half
    D. *good* because the one sling can be placed faster than the two

11._____

12. The wrench that would prove LEAST useful in uncoupling several pieces of pipe is a _____ wrench.

    A. socket   B. chain   C. strap   D. stillson

12._____

13. Concrete (a mixture of cement, sand and coarse aggregate), if made from 1 part of one material, 3 parts of a second material and 5 parts of the remaining material, is known as 1:3:5 concrete. It would be LOGICAL to conclude that the parts would be

    A. 1 cement, 3 coarse aggregate, 5 sand
    B. 1 coarse aggregate, 3 cement, 5 sand
    C. 1 sand, 3 coarse aggregate, 5 cement
    D. 1 cement, 3 sand, 5 coarse aggregate

13._____

14. Gaskets are commonly used between the flanges of large pipe joints to

    A. provide space for assembly
    B. take up expansion and contraction
    C. prevent the flanges from rusting together
    D. make a tight connection

14._____

15. If you do NOT understand the operation of some special tool which is used in your work, your BEST procedure would be to

    A. study up on its operation at home
    B. ask a maintainer to explain its operation
    C. ask another helper to explain its operation
    D. bother nobody and expect to pick up a little more knowledge each time you use the tool

15._____

16. The number of board feet in a piece of lumber is equal to the cross-sectional area in square inches divided by 12 and multiplied by the length of the piece in feet. Therefore, among four different pieces of lumber of equal length, the GREATEST number of board feet would be in the piece whose other two dimensions are

    A. 1" x 12"   B. 2" x 10"   C. 3" x 8"   D. 4" x 4"

16._____

17. When sandpapering wood by hand, the sanding should be done

    A. with the grain   B. across the grain
    C. diagonally to the grain   D. with a circular motion

17._____

18. A drift pin is used to

    A. line up holes   B. set nails
    C. enlarge holes   D. keep a nut from turning

18._____

19. Holes are *usually* countersunk when installing

    A. carriage bolts
    B. lag screws
    C. flat-head screws
    D. square nuts

20. Of the following, the tool that is LEAST easily broken is a

    A. file
    B. pry bar
    C. folding rule
    D. hacksaw blade

21. A hacksaw blade having 32 teeth to the inch is the BEST blade to use when cutting

    A. cold rolled steel shafting
    B. wrought iron pipe
    C. stainless steel plate
    D. copper tubing

22. The joints in long vertical supporting timbers of wooden scaffolds are made with the timbers butted, rather than lapped, *principally* because this results in

    A. better appearance
    B. more resistance to the weather
    C. lighter timbers
    D. less strain on the nails

23. Practically all valves used in plumbing work are made so that the hand wheel is turned clockwise instead of counterclockwise to close the valve. The *probable* reason is that

    A. the hand wheel is less likely to loosen
    B. it is easier to remember since screws and nuts move inward when turned clockwise
    C. greater force can be exerted
    D. most poeple are right handed

24. The transit authority gives some of its maintenance employees instruction in first aid. The MOST likely reason for doing this is to

    A. eliminate the need for calling a doctor in case of accident
    B. reduce the number of accidents
    C. lower the cost of accidents to the transit authority
    D. provide temporary first aid

25. Wooden platforms on elevated stations are built of 2" x 6" planks with a small opening between the planks. The purpose of this construction is to

    A. provide for drainage
    B. create a more attractive design
    C. provide a non-slip surface
    D. use less lumber for a given area

26. In order to determine the exact location of a leak in an air hose from a portable compressor, you should

    A. paint the suspected area with soap suds
    B. test with a lighted match

C. cut fine strips of paper and hold them near the location
D. hold your ear close to the hose

27. After No. 20, the next smaller twist drill size is No.

 A. 18 B. 19 C. 21 D. 22

28. If you had to telephone for an ambulance because of an accident, the MOST important information for you to give the person who answered the telephone would be the

 A. exact time of the accident
 B. place where the ambulance is needed
 C. cause of the accident
 D. names and addresses of those injured

29. Good practice dictates that an adjustable open-end wrench should be used *primarily* when the

 A. nut to be turned is soft and must not be scored
 B. extra leverage is needed
 C. proper size of fixed wrench is not available
 D. location is cramped permitting only a small turning angle

30. The ends of a length of manila rope are "whipped" (wrapped with thin twine) in order to

 A. make the rope more flexible
 B. prevent the strands from unraveling
 C. prevent rotting of the ends
 D. reduce the diameter of the rope at the ends

KEY (CORRECT ANSWERS)

1. B
2. A
3. C
4. B
5. C

6. A
7. C
8. C
9. B
10. A

11. A/B
12. A
13. D
14. D
15. B

16. C
17. A
18. A
19. C
20. B

21. D
22. D
23. B
24. D
25. A

26. A/D
27. C
28. B
29. C
30. B

EXAMINATION SECTION
TEST 1

DIRECTIONS: Each question or incomplete statement is followed by several suggested answers or completions. Select the one that BEST answers the question or completes the statement. *PRINT THE LETTER OF THE CORRECT ANSWER IN THE SPACE AT THE RIGHT.*

1.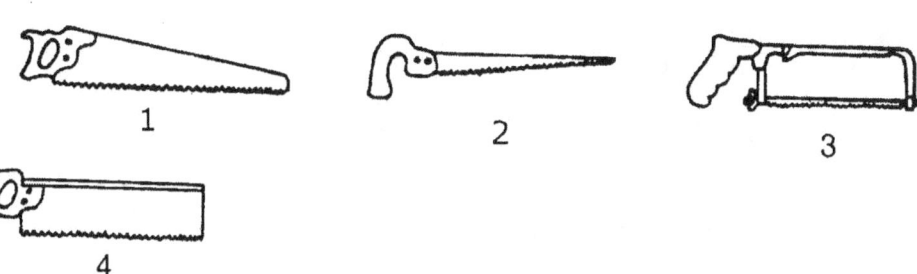

   The saw that is used PRINCIPALLY where curved cuts are to be made is numbered

   A. 1   B. 2   C. 3   D. 4

   1.____

2.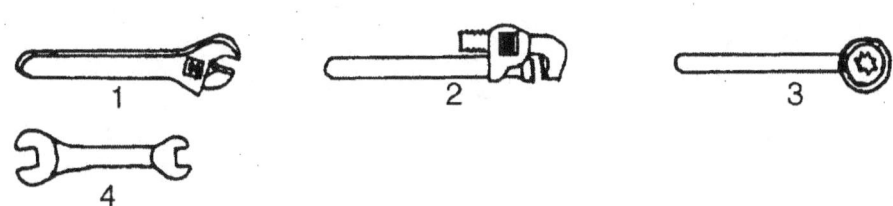

   The wrench that is used PRINCIPALLY for pipe work is numbered

   A. 1   B. 2   C. 3   D. 4

   2.____

3.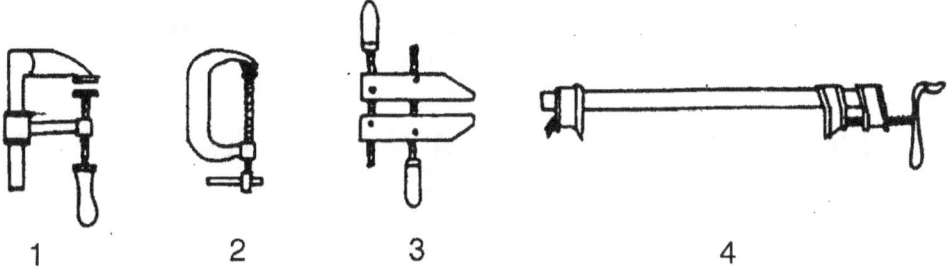

   The carpenter's *hand screw* is numbered

   A. 1   B. 2   C. 3   D. 4

   3.____

4.

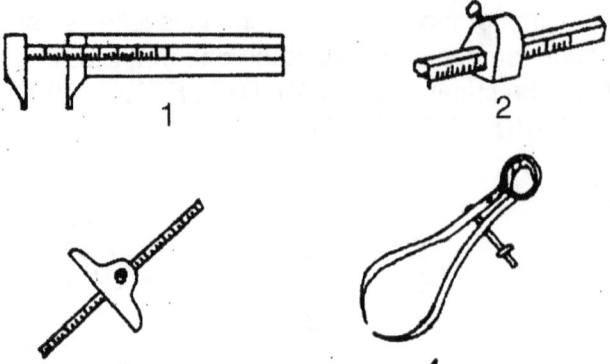

The tool used to measure the depth of a hole is numbered

A. 1 B. 2 C. 3 D. 4

5.

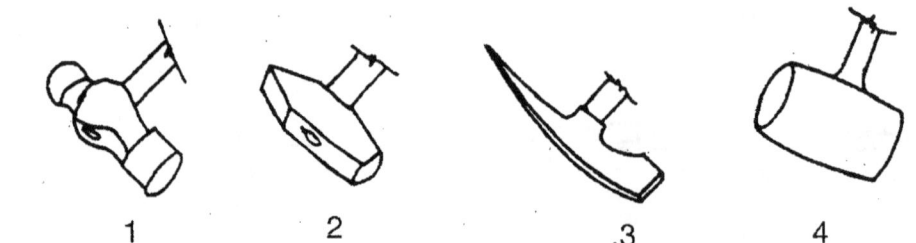

The tool that is BEST suited for use with a wood chisel is numbered

A. 1 B. 2 C. 3 D. 4

6.

The screw head that would be tightened with an *Allen* wrench is numbered

A. 1 B. 2 C. 3 D. 4

7.

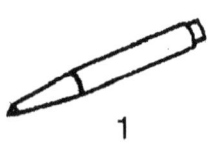 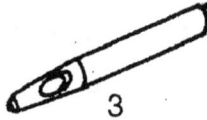

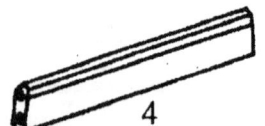

The center punch is numbered

A. 1 B. 2 C. 3 D. 4

8.

The tool used to drill a hole in concrete is numbered

   A. 1   B. 2   C. 3   D. 4

9.

The wrench whose PRINCIPAL purpose to to hold taps for threading is numbered

   A. 1   B. 2   C. 3   D. 4

10.

The electrician's bit is indicated by the number

   A. 1   B. 2   C. 3   D. 4

11. The ends of a joist in a brick building are cut to a bevel. This is done PRINCIPALLY to prevent damage to

   A. joist   B. floor   C. sill   D. wall

12. Of the following, the wood that is MOST commonly used today for floor joists is   12._____

    A. long leaf yellow pine   B. douglas fir
    C. oak   D. birch

13. Quarter-sawed lumber is preferred for the BEST finished flooring PRINCIPALLY because it   13._____

    A. has the greatest strength   B. shrinks the least
    C. is the easiest to nail   D. is the easiest to handle

14. A tool used in hanging doors is a   14._____

    A. miter gauge   B. line level
    C. try square   D. butt gauge

15. Of the following, the MAXIMUM height that would be considered acceptable for a stair riser is   15._____

    A. 6 1/2"   B. 7 1/2"   C. 8 1/2"   D. 9 1/2"

16. The PRINCIPAL reason for *cross banding* the layers of wood in a plywood panel is to _____ of the panel.   16._____

    A. reduce warping   B. increase the strength
    C. reduce the cost   D. increase the beauty

17. The part of a tree that will produce the DENSEST wood is the _____ wood.   17._____

    A. spring   B. summer   C. sap   D. heart

18. Casing nails MOST NEARLY resemble _____ nails.   18._____

    A. common   B. roofing   C. form   D. finishing

19. Lumber in quantity is ordered by   19._____

    A. cubic feet   B. foot board measure
    C. lineal feet   D. weight and length

20. For finishing of wood, BEST results are obtained by sanding   20._____

    A. with a circular motion
    B. against the grain
    C. with the grain
    D. with a circular motion on edges and against the grain on the flat parts

21. A *chase* in a brick wall is a   21._____

    A. pilaster   B. waterstop   C. recess   D. corbel

22. Parging refers to   22._____

    A. increasing the thickness of a brick wall
    B. plastering the back of face brickwork
    C. bonding face brick to backing blocks
    D. leveling each course of brick

23. The PRINCIPAL reason for requiring brick to be wetted before laying is that 23.____

    A. less water is required in the mortar
    B. efflorescence is prevented
    C. the brick will not absorb as much water from the mortar
    D. cool brick is easier to handle

24. In brickwork, muriatic acid is commonly used to 24.____

    A. increase the strength of the mortar
    B. etch the brick
    C. waterproof the wall
    D. clean the wall

25. Cement mortar can be made easier to work by the addition of a small quantity of 25.____

    A. lime   B. soda   C. litharge   D. plaster

26. Headers in brickwork are used to _____ the wall. 26.____

    A. strengthen   B. reduce the cost of
    C. speed the erection of   D. align

27. Joints in brick walls are tooled 27.____

    A. immediately after each brick is laid
    B. after the mortar has had its initial set
    C. after the entire wall is completed
    D. 28 days after the wall has been built

28. If cement mortar has begun to set before it can be used in a wall, the BEST thing to do is to 28.____

    A. use the mortar immediately as is
    B. add a small quantity of lime
    C. add some water and mix thoroughly
    D. discard the mortar

29. A *bat* in brickwork is a 29.____

    A. brace to hold a wall temporarily in place
    B. stick used to aid in mixing of mortar
    C. broken piece of brick used to fill short spaces
    D. curved brick used in ornamental work

30. The proportions by volume of cement, lime, and sand in a cement-lime mortar should be, according to the Building Code, 30.____

    A. 1:1:3   B. 2:1:6   C. 1:1:6   D. 1:2:6

31. The BEST flux to use when soldering galvanized iron is 31.____

    A. killed acid   B. sal-ammoniac
    C. muriatic acid   D. resin

32. When soldering a vertical joint, the soldering iron should be tinned on _____ side(s). 32._____
    A. 1   B. 2   C. 3   D. 4

33. The difference between *right hand* and *left hand* tin snips is the 33._____
    A. relative position of the cutting jaws
    B. shape of the cutting jaws
    C. shape of the handles
    D. relative position of the handles

34. A machine used to bend sheet metal is called a 34._____
    A. router   B. planer   C. brake   D. swage

35. The type of solder that would be used in *hard soldering* would be _____ solder. 35._____
    A. bismuth   B. wiping   C. 50-50   D. silver

36. Roll roofing material is usually felt which has been impregnated with 36._____
    A. cement   B. mastic   C. tar   D. latex

37. The purpose of flashing on roofs is to 37._____
    A. secure roofing materials to the roof
    B. make it easier to lay the roofing
    C. prevent leaks through the roof
    D. insulate the roof from excessive heat

38. The tool used to spread hot pitch on a three-ply roofing job is a 38._____
    A. mop   B. spreader C. pusher   D. broom

39. The cutting of glass can be facilitated by dipping the cutting wheel in 39._____
    A. *3-in-1* oil B. water C. lard D. kerosene

40. The strips of metal used to hold glass to the window frame while it is being puttied are called 40._____
    A. hold-downs   B. points   C. wedges   D. triangles

41. The type of chain used with sash weights is _____ link. 41._____
    A. flat   B. round
    C. figure-eight   D. basket-weave

42. The material that would be used to seal around a window frame is 42._____
    A. oakum   B. litharge C. grout   D. calking

43. The function of a window sill is MOST NEARLY the same as that of a 43._____
    A. jamb   B. coping   C. lintel   D. brick

44. Lightweight plaster would be made with 44._____
    A. sand   B. cinders   C. potash   D. vermiculite

66

45. The FIRST coat of plaster to be applied on a three-coat plaster job is the _____ coat. 45.____

    A. brown B. scratch C. white D. keene

46. Screeds in plaster work are used to 46.____

    A. remove larger sizes of sand
    B. hold the batch of plaster before it is applied
    C. apply the plaster to the wall
    D. guide the plasterer in making, an even wall

47. The FIRST coat of plaster over rock lath should be a _____ plaster. 47.____

    A. gypsum B. lime
    C. portland cement D. puzzolan cement

48. In plastering, a *hawk* is used to _____ plaster. 48.____

    A. apply B. hold C. scratch D. smooth

49. When mixing concrete by hand, the order in which the ingredients should be mixed is: 49.____

    A. water, cement, sand, stone
    B. sand, cement, water, stone
    C. stone, water, sand, cement
    D. stone, sand, cement, water

50. The PRINCIPAL reason for covering a concrete sidewalk with straw or paper after the concrete has been poured is to 50.____

    A. prevent people from walking on the concrete while it is still wet
    B. impart a rough non-slip surface to the concrete
    C. prevent excessive evaporation of water in the concrete
    D. shorten the length of time it would take for the concrete to harden

KEY (CORRECT ANSWERS)

1. B	11. D	21. C	31. C	41. A
2. B	12. B	22. B	32. A	42. D
3. C	13. B	23. C	33. A	43. B
4. C	14. D	24. D	34. C	44. D
5. D	15. B	25. A	35. D	45. B
6. C	16. A	26. A	36. C	46. D
7. A	17. D	27. B	37. C	47. A
8. D	18. D	28. D	38. A	48. B
9. A	19. B	29. C	39. D	49. D
10. C	20. C	30. C	40. B	50. C

TEST 2

DIRECTIONS: Each question or incomplete statement is followed by several suggested answers or completions. Select the one that BEST answers the question or completes the statement. *PRINT THE LETTER OF THE CORRECT ANSWER IN THE SPACE AT THE RIGHT.*

1. When colored concrete is required, the colors used should be 1._____

    A. colors in oil
    B. mineral pigments
    C. tempera colors
    D. water colors

2. Concrete is *rubbed* with a(n) 2._____

    A. emery wheel
    B. carborundum brick
    C. sandstone
    D. alundum stick

3. To prevent concrete from sticking to forms, the forms should be painted with 3._____

    A. oil   B. kerosene   C. water   D. lime

4. The reinforcement in a concrete floor slab is referred to as 6"-6" x #6-#6. The type of reinforcing that is being used is 4._____

    A. steel bars
    B. wire mesh
    C. angle irons
    D. grating plate

5. One method of measuring the consistency of a concrete mix is by means of a _____ test. 5._____

    A. penetration   B. flow   C. slump   D. weight

6. A chemical that is sometimes used to prevent the freezing of concrete in cold weather is 6._____

    A. alum
    B. glycerine
    C. calcium chloride
    D. sodium nitrate

7. The one of the following that is LEAST commonly used for columns is 7._____

    A. wide flange beams
    B. angles
    C. concrete-filled pipe
    D. *I* beams

8. Fire protection of steel floor beams is MOST frequently accomplished by the use of 8._____

    A. gypsum block
    B. brick
    C. rock wool fill
    D. vermiculite gypsum plaster

9. A *Pittsburgh lock* is a(n) 9._____

    A. emergency door lock
    B. sheet metal joint
    C. elevator safety
    D. boiler valve

10. In order to drill a hole at right angle to the horizontal axis of a round bar, the bar should be held in a 10._____

    A. step block
    B. C-block
    C. hand pliers
    D. V-block

11. The procedure to follow in the lubrication of maintenance shop equipment is to lubricate   11._____

    A. when you can spare the time
    B. only when necessary
    C. at regular intervals
    D. when the equipment is in operation

12. Of the following items, the one which is NOT used in making fastenings to masonry or plaster walls is a(n)   12._____

    A. lead shield   B. expansion bolt
    C. rawl plug   D. steel bushing

13. When a common straight ladder is used to paint a wall, the safe distance that the foot of the ladder should be set away from the wall is MOST NEARLY _____ the length of the ladder.   13._____

    A. one-eighth   B. one-quarter
    C. one-half   D. five-eighths

14. The term *bell and spigot* usually refers to   14._____

    A. refrigerator motors   B. cast iron pipes
    C. steam radiator outlets D. electrical receptacles

15. In plumbing work, a valve which allows water to flow in one direction only is commonly known as a _____ valve.   15._____

    A. check   B. globe   C. gate   D. stop

16. A pipe coupling is BEST used to connect two pieces of pipe of   16._____

    A. the same diameter in a straight line
    B. the same diameter at right angles to each other
    C. different diameters at a 45° angle
    D. different diameters at an 1/8th bend

17. A fitting or pipe with many outlets relatively close together is commonly called a   17._____

    A. manifold   B. gooseneck
    C. flange union   D. return bend

18. To locate the center in the end of a sound shaft, the BEST tool to use is a(n)   18._____

    A. ruler   B. divider
    C. hermaphrodite caliper D. micrometer

19. When cutting a piece of 1 1/4" O.D. 20 gauge brass tubing with a hand hacksaw, it is BEST to use a blade having _____ teeth per inch.   19._____

    A. 14   B. 18   C. 22   D. 32

20. When cutting a piece of 1" O.D. extra-heavy pipe with a pipe cutter, a burr usually forms on the inside and the outside of the pipe. These burrs are BEST removed by means of a pipe   20._____

    A. tap and a file   B. wrench and rough stone
    C. reamer and a file   D. drill and a chisel

21. Artificial respiration should be started immediately on a man who has suffered an electric shock if he is

   A. *unconscious* and breathing
   B. *unconscious* and not breathing
   C. *conscious* and in a daze
   D. *conscious* and badly burned

22. The fuse of a certain circuit has blown and is replaced with a fuse of the same rating which also blows when the switch is closed.
   In this case,

   A. a fuse of higher current rating should be used
   B. a fuse of higher voltage rating should be used
   C. the fuse should be temporarily replaced by a heavy piece of wire
   D. the circuit should be checked

23. Operating an incandescent electric light bulb at less than its rated voltage will result in

   A. shorter life and brighter light
   B. longer life and dimmer light
   C. brighter light and longer life
   D. dimmer light and shorter life

24. In order to control a lamp from two different positions, it is necessary to use

   A. two single pole switches
   B. one single pole switch and one four-way switch
   C. two three-way switches
   D. one single pole switch and one four-way switch

25.

One method of testing fuses is to connect a pair of test lamps in the circuit in such a manner that the test lamp will light up if the fuse is good and will remain dark if the fuse is bad. In the above illustration 1 and 2 are fuses.
In order to test if fuse 1 is bad, test lamps should be connected between

   A. A and B   B. B and D   C. A and D   D. C and B

26. The PRINCIPAL reason for the grounding of electrical equipment and circuits is to

   A. prevent short circuits   B. insure safety from shock
   C. save power   D. increase voltage

27. The ordinary single-pole flush wall type switch must be connected

    A. across the line
    B. in the *hot* conductor
    C. in the grounded conductor
    D. in the white conductor

28. A D.C. shunt motor runs in the wrong direction. This fault can be CORRECTED by

    A. reversing the connections of both the field and the armature
    B. interchanging the connections of either main or auxiliar windings
    C. interchanging the connections to either the field or the armature windings
    D. interchanging the connections to the line of the power leads

29. The MOST common type of motor that can be used with both A.C. and D.C. sources is the _____ motor.

    A. compound   B. repulsion   C. series   D. shunt

30. A fluorescent fixture in a new building has been in use for several months without trouble. Recently, the ends of the fluorscent lamp have remained lighted when the light was switched off.
    The BEST way to clear up this trouble is to replace the

    A. lamp   B. ballast   C. starter   D. sockets

31. The BEST wood to use for handles of tools such as axes and hammers is

    A. hemlock   B. pine   C. oak   D. hickory

32. A *hanger bolt*

    A. has a square head
    B. is bent in a *U* shape
    C. has a different type of thread at each end
    D. is threaded the entire length from point to head

33. A stone frequently used to sharpen tools is

    A. carborundum   B. bauxite   C. resin   D. slate

34. A strike plate is MOST closely associated with a

    A. lock   B. sash   C. butt   D. tie rod

35. The material that distinguishes a terrazzo floor from an ordinary concrete floor is

    A. cinders
    B. marble chip
    C. cut stone
    D. non-slip aggregate

36. A room is 7'6" wide by 9'0" long with a ceiling height of 8'0". One gallon of flat paint will cover approximately 400 square feet of wall.
    The number of gallons of this paint required to paint the walls of this room, making no deductions for windows or doors, is MOST NEARLY _____ gallon.

    A. 1/4   B. 1/2   C. 3/4   D. 1

37. The cost of a certain job is broken down as follows:
    Materials $375
    Rental of equipment 120
    Labor   315
    The percentage of the total cost of the job that can be charged to materials is MOST NEARLY

    A. 40%   B. 42%   C. 44%   D. 46%

38. By trial, it is found that by using two cubic feet of sand, a five cubic foot batch of concrete is produced.
    Using the same proportions, the amount of sand required to produce 2 cubic yards of concrete is MOST NEARLY _____ cu.ft.

    A. 20   B. 22   C. 24   D. 26

39. It takes 4 men 6 days to do a certain job.
    Working at the same speed, the number of days it will take 3 men to do this job is

    A. 7   B. 8   C. 9   D. 10

40. The cost of rawl plugs is $2.75 per gross. The cost of 2,448 rawl plugs is

    A. $46.75   B. $47.25   C. $47.75   D. $48.25

41. *Rigidity* of the hammer handle enables the operator to control and direct the force of the blow.
    As used above, *rigidity* means MOST NEARLY

    A. straightness   B. strength
    C. shape   D. stiffness

42. *For precision work, center punches are ground to a fine tapered point.* As used above, *tapered* means MOST NEARLY

    A. conical   B. straight   C. accurate   D. smooth

43. There are *limitations* to the drilling of metals by hand power.
    As used above, *limitations* means MOST NEARLY

    A. advantages   B. restrictions
    C. difficulties   D. benefits

Questions 44-45.

DIRECTIONS: Questions 44 and 45 are based on the following paragraph.

Because electric drills run at high speed, the cutting edges of a twist drill are heated quickly. If the metal is thick, the drill point must be withdrawn from the hole frequently to cool it and clear out chips. Forcing the drill continuously into a deep hole will heat it, thereby spoiling its temper and cutting edges. A portable electric drill has the advantage that it can be taken to the work and used to drill holes in material too large to handle in a drill press.

44. According to the above paragraph, overheating of a twist drill will

    A. slow down the work   B. cause excessive drill breakage
    C. dull the drill   D. spoil the accuracy of the work

45. According to the above paragraph, one method of preventing overheating of a twist drill is to

   A. use cooling oil
   B. drill a smaller pilot hole first
   C. use a drill press
   D. remove the drill from the work frequently

Questions 46-50.

DIRECTIONS: Questions 46 to 50 are to be answered in accordance with the sketch shown below.

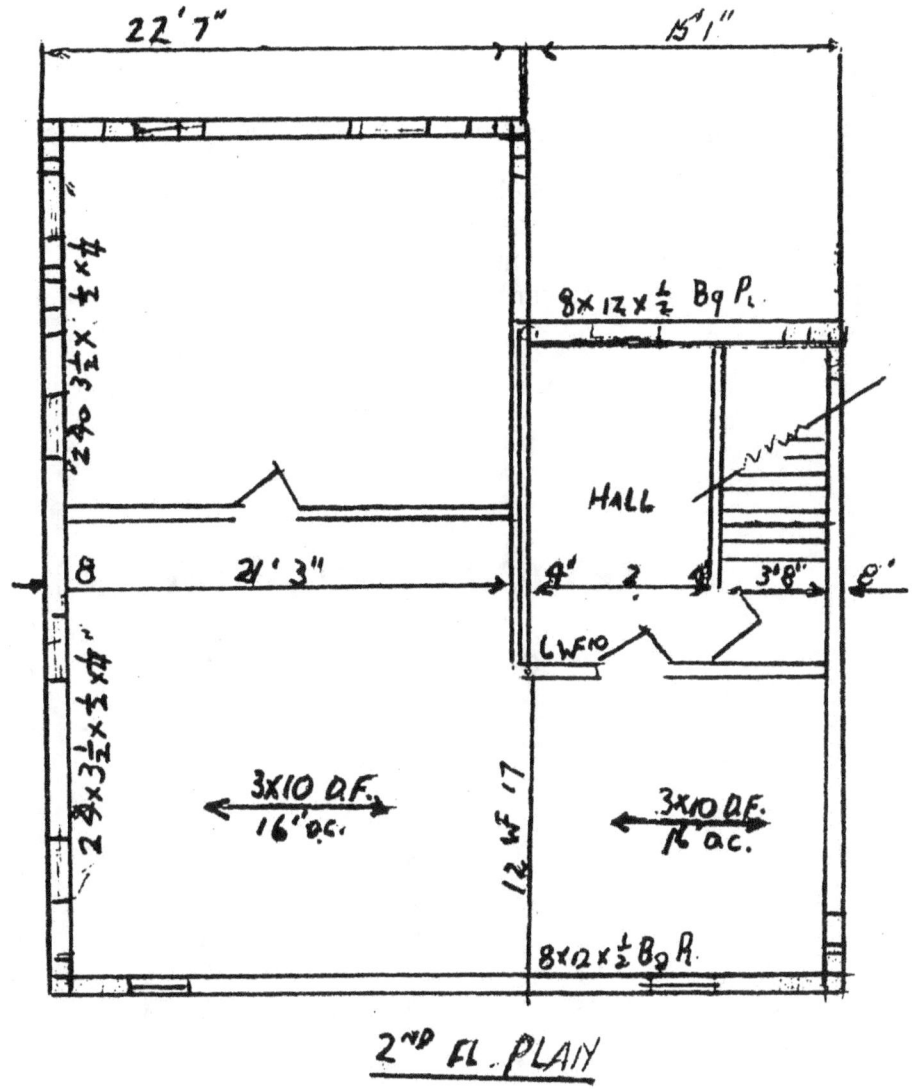

2ND FL. PLAN

46. The one of the following statements that is CORRECT is the building

   A. is of fireproof construction
   B. has masonry walls with wood joists
   C. is of wood frame construction
   D. has timber joists and girders

47. The one of the following statements that is CORRECT is

    A. the stairway from the ground continues through the roof
    B. there are two means of egress from the second floor of this building
    C. the door on the second floor stair landing opens in the direction of egress
    D. the entire stair is shown on this plan

48. The width of the hall is

    A. 10'3"   B. 10'5"   C. 10'7"   D. 10'9"

49. The lintels shown are

    A. angles
    C. an I-beam
    B. a channel and an angle
    D. precast concrete

50. The one of the following statements that is CORRECT is that the steel beam is

    A. supported by columns at the center and at the ends
    B. entirely supported by the walls
    C. supported on columns at the ends only
    D. supported at the center by a column and at the ends by the walls

KEY (CORRECT ANSWERS)

1. B	11. C	21. B	31. D	41. D
2. B	12. D	22. D	32. C	42. A
3. A	13. B	23. B	33. A	43. B
4. B	14. B	24. C	34. A	44. C
5. C	15. A	25. C	35. B	45. D
6. C	16. A	26. B	36. C	46. B
7. B	17. A	27. B	37. D	47. C
8. D	18. C	28. C	38. B	48. D
9. B	19. D	29. C	39. B	49. A
10. D	20. C	30. C	40. A	50. D

EXAMINATION SECTION
TEST 1

DIRECTIONS: Each question or incomplete statement is followed by several suggested answers or completions. Select the one that BEST answers the question or completes the statement. *PRINT THE LETTER OF THE CORRECT ANSWER IN THE SPACE AT THE RIGHT.*

1. Linseed oil putty would MOST likely be used to secure glass in _____ windows. 1.____

    A. steel casement B. aluminum jalousie
    C. wood double hung D. aluminum storm

2. Of the following, the one type of glass that should NOT be cut with the ordinary type glass cutter is _____ glass. 2.____

    A. safety B. plate C. wire D. herculite

3. Thermopane is made of two sheets of glass separated by 3.____

    A. a sheet of celluloid B. wire mesh
    C. an air space D. mica

4. Glass is NEVER cut so that it fits snugly inside the frame of a steel casement window. Of the following, the MAIN reason for allowing this space between the glass and the side of the frame is to 4.____

    A. prevent cracking of the glass in cold weather
    B. permit the glass to be lined up properly
    C. allow space for the putty
    D. eliminate the necessity of polishing the edges of the glass

5. Glass is held in steel sash by means of 5.____

    A. points B. clips C. plates D. blocks

6. When nailing felt to a roof, the nails should be driven through a 6.____

    A. tinned disc B. steel washer
    C. brass plate D. plastic bushing

7. An opening in a parapet wall for draining water from a roof is MOST often called a 7.____

    A. leader B. gutter C. downspout D. scupper

8. Roofing nails are usually 8.____

    A. brass B. cement coated
    C. galvanized D. nickel plated

9. A *street ell* is a fitting having 9.____

    A. male threads at both ends
    B. male threads at one end and female threads at the other end
    C. female threads at both ends
    D. male threads at one end and a solder connection at the other end

10. Of the following pieces of equipment, the one on which you would MOST likely find a safety (pop-off) valve is a(n)

    A. hot air furnace
    B. air conditioning compressor
    C. hot water heater
    D. dehumidifier

11. Compression fittings are MOST often used with

    A. cast iron bell and spigot pipe
    B. steel flange pipe
    C. copper tubing
    D. transite

12. Water hammer is BEST eliminated by

    A. increasing the size of all the piping
    B. installing an air chamber
    C. replacing the valve seats with neoprene gaskets
    D. flushing the system to remove corrosion

13. The BEST type of pipe to use in a gas line in a domestic installation is

    A. black iron
    B. galvanized iron
    C. cast iron
    D. wrought steel

14. If there is a pinhole in the float of a toilet tank, the

    A. water will flush continually
    B. toilet cannot flush
    C. tank cannot be filled with water
    D. valve will not shut off so water will overflow into the overflow tube

15. Condensation of moisture in humid weather occurs MOST often on _____ pipe(s).

    A. sewage
    B. gas
    C. hot water
    D. cold water

16. A gas appliance should be connected to a gas line by means of a(n)

    A. union
    B. right and left coupling
    C. elbow
    D. close nipple

17. A PRINCIPAL difference between a pipe thread and a machine thread is that the pipe thread is

    A. tapered   B. finer   C. flat   D. longer

18. When joining galvanized iron pipe, pipe joint compound is placed on

    A. the female threads only
    B. the male threads only
    C. both the male and female threads
    D. either the male or the female threads depending on the type of fitting

19. If moisture is trapped between the layers of a 3-ply roof, the heat of a summer day will

    A. dry the roof out
    B. cause blisters to be formed in the roofing
    C. rot the felt material
    D. have no effect on the roofing

20. Of the following, the metal MOST often used for leaders and gutters is

    A. monel   B. brass
    C. steel   D. galvanized iron

21. When drilling a small hole in sheet copper, the BEST practice is to

    A. make a dent with a center punch first
    B. put some cutting oil at the point you intend to drill
    C. use a slow speed drill to prevent overheating
    D. use an auger type bit

22. The reason for annealing sheet copper is to make it

    A. soft and easier to work
    B. more resistant to weather
    C. easier to solder
    D. harder and more resistant to blows

23. In draw filing,

    A. only the edge of the file is used
    B. a triangle file is generally used
    C. the file is pulled toward the mechanic's body in filing
    D. the file must have a safe edge

24. The type of paint that uses water as a thinner is

    A. enamel   B. latex   C. shellac   D. lacquer

25. The reason for placing a 6" sub-base of cinders under a concrete sidewalk is to

    A. provide flexibility in the surface
    B. permit drainage of water
    C. prevent chemicals in the soil from damaging the sidewalk
    D. allow room for the concrete to expand

26. The BEST material to use to lubricate a door lock is

    A. penetrating oil   B. pike oil
    C. graphite   D. light grease

27. Assume that the color of the flame from a gas stove is bright yellow. To correct this, you should

    A. close the air flap
    B. open the air flap
    C. increase the gas pressure
    D. increase the size of the gas opening

28. In a 110-220 volt three-wire circuit, the neutral wire is usually

   A. black   B. red   C. white   D. green

29. Brushes on fractional horsepower universal motors are MOST often made of

   A. flexible copper strands
   B. rigid carbon blocks
   C. thin wire strips
   D. collector rings

30. Leaks from the stem of a faucet can generally be stopped by replacing the

   A. bibb washer   B. seat   C. packing   D. gasket

31. Of the following, the BEST procedure to follow with a frozen water pipe is to

   A. allow the pipe to thaw out by itself as the weather gets warmer
   B. put anti-freeze into the pipe above the section that is frozen
   C. turn on the hot water heater
   D. open the faucet closest to the frozen pipe and warm the pipe with a blow torch, starting at this point

32. The one of the following that is NOT usually changed by a central air conditioning system is the

   A. volume of air in the system
   B. humidity of the air
   C. dust in the air
   D. air pressure of the system

33. The temperature of a domestic hot water system is MOST often controlled by a(n)

   A. relief valve   B. aquastat   C. barometer   D. thermostat

34. Draft in a chimney is MOST often controlled by a(n)

   A. damper
   B. gate
   C. orifice
   D. cross connection

35. Assume that a refrigerator motor operates continuously for excessively long periods of time.
   The FIRST item you should check to locate the defect is the

   A. plug in the outlet
   B. door gasket
   C. direction of rotation of the motor
   D. motor switch

36. Assume that after replacing a defective motor for a large electric fan, you find that the fan is rotating in the wrong direction.
   If the motor is a split phase motor, with the shaft at one end only, the trouble could be CORRECTED by

   A. reversing the fan on its shaft
   B. turning the motor end for end
   C. interchanging the connections on the field terminals of the motor
   D. reversing the plug in the electric outlet

37. In order to properly hang a door, shims are frequently inserted under the hinges. These shims are MOST often made of

    A. cardboard
    B. sheet steel
    C. bakelite
    D. the same materials as the hinges

38. Flooring nails are usually _____ nails.

    A. casing   B. common   C. cut   D. clinch

39. Over a doorway, to support brick, you will usually find

    A. steel angles   B. hanger bolts
    C. wooden headers   D. stirrups

40. Insulation of steam pipes is MOST often done with

    A. asbestos   B. celotex   C. alundum   D. sheathing

41. Assume that only the first few coils of a hot water convector used for heating a room are hot.
    To correct this, you should FIRST

    A. increase the water pressure
    B. increase the water temperature
    C. bleed the air out of the convector
    D. clean the convector pipes

42. The MAIN reason for grounding the outer sheel of an electric fixture is to

    A. provide additional support for the fixture
    B. reduce the cost of installation of the fixture
    C. provide a terminal to which the wires can be attached
    D. reduce the chance of electric shock

43. In woodwork, countersinking is MOST often done for

    A. lag screws   B. carriage bolts
    C. hanger bolts   D. flat head screws

44. Bridging is MOST often used in connection with

    A. door frames   B. window openings
    C. floor joists   D. stud walls

45. A saddle is part of a

    A. doorway   B. window
    C. stair well   D. bulkhead

46. To make it easier to drive screws into hard wood, it is BEST to   46.____

    A. use a screwdriver that is longer than that used for soft wood
    B. rub the threads of the screw on a bar of soap
    C. oil the screw threads
    D. use a square shank screwdriver assisted by a wrench

47. In using a doweled joint to make a repair of a wooden door, it is important to remember that the dowel   47.____

    A. hole must be smaller in diameter than the dowel so that there is a tight fit
    B. hole must be longer than the dowel to provide a room for excess glue
    C. must be of the same type of wood as the door frame
    D. must be held in place by a small screw while waiting for the glue to set

48. The edges of MOST finished wood flooring are   48.____

    A. tongue and groove
    B. mortise and tenon
    C. bevel and miter
    D. lap and scarf

49. For the SMOOTHEST finish, sanding of wood should be done   49.____

    A. in a circular direction
    B. diagonally against the grain
    C. across the grain
    D. parallel with the grain

50. To prevent splintering of wood when boring a hole through it, the BEST practice is to   50.____

    A. drill at a slow speed
    B. use a scrap piece to back up the work
    C. use an auger bit
    D. ease up the pressure on the drill when the drill is almost through the wood

KEY (CORRECT ANSWERS)

1. C	11. C	21. A	31. D	41. C
2. D	12. B	22. A	32. D	42. D
3. C	13. A	23. C	33. B	43. D
4. A	14. D	24. B	34. A	44. C
5. B	15. D	25. B	35. B	45. A
6. A	16. B	26. C	36. C	46. B
7. D	17. A	27. B	37. A	47. B
8. C	18. B	28. C	38. C	48. A
9. B	19. B	29. B	39. A	49. D
10. C	20. D	30. C	40. A	50. B

TEST 2

DIRECTIONS: Each question or incomplete statement is followed by several suggested answers or completions. Select the one that BEST answers the question or completes the statement. *PRINT THE LETTER OF THE CORRECT ANSWER IN THE SPACE AT THE RIGHT.*

1. A *speed nut* has

    A. no threads
    B. threads that are coarser than a standard nut
    C. threads that are finer than s standard nut
    D. fewer threads than a standard nut

    1.____

2. The BEST tool to use to remove the burr and sharp edge resulting from cutting tubing with a tube cutter is a

    A. file   B. scraper   C. reamer   D. knife

    2.____

3. A router is used PRINCIPALLY to

    A. clean pipe
    B. cut grooves in wood
    C. bend electric conduit
    D. sharpen tools

    3.____

4. The principle of operation of a sabre saw is MOST similar to that of a _____ saw.

    A. circular   B. radial   C. swing   D. jig

    4.____

5. A full thread cutting set would have both taps and

    A. cutters   B. bushings   C. dies   D. plugs

    5.____

6. The proper flux to use for soldering electric wire connections is

    A. rosin
    B. killed acid
    C. borax
    D. zinc chloride

    6.____

7. A fusestat differs from an ordinary plug fuse in that a fusestat has

    A. less current carrying capacity
    B. different size threads
    C. an aluminum shell instead of a copper shell
    D. no threads

    7.____

8. A grounding type 120-volt receptacle differs from an ordinary electric receptacle MAINLY in that a grounding receptacle

    A. is larger than the ordinary receptacle
    B. has openings for a three prong plug
    C. can be used for larger machinery
    D. has a built-in circuit breaker

    8.____

9. A carbide tip is MOST often found on a bit used for drilling

    A. concrete   B. wood   C. steel   D. brass

    9.____

10. The MAIN reason for using oil on an oilstone is to

    A. make the surface of the stone smoother
    B. prevent clogging of the pores of the stone
    C. reduce the number of times the stone has to be *dressed*
    D. prevent gouging of the stone's surface

11. The sum of the following numbers, 1 3/4, 3 1/6, 5 1/2, 6 5/8, and 9 1/4, is

    A. 26 1/8   B. 26 1/4   C. 26 1/2   D. 26 3/4

12. If a piece of plywood measures 5' 1 1/4" x 3' 2 1/2", the number of square feet in this board is MOST NEARLY

    A. 15.8   B. 16.1   C. 16.4   D. 16.7

13. Assume that in quantity purchases the city receives a discount of 33 1/3%.
    If a one gallon can of paint retails at $5.33 per gallon, the cost of 375 gallons of this paint is MOST NEARLY

    A. $1,332.50   B. $1,332.75   C. $1,333.00   D. $1,333.25

14. Assume that eight barrels of cement together weigh a total of 3004 lbs. and 12 oz.
    If there are four bags of cement per barrel, then the weight of one bag of cement is MOST NEARLY _____ lbs.

    A. 93.1   B. 93.5   C. 93.9   D. 94.3

15. Assume that one man cuts 50 nameplates per hour, whereas his co-worker cuts 55 nameplates per hour.
    At the end of 7 hours, the first man will have cut fewer nameplates than the second man by

    A. 9.3%   B. 9.5%   C. 9.7%   D. 9.9%

16. Under the same conditions, the one of the following that dries the FASTEST is

    A. shellac   B. varnish   C. enamel   D. lacquer

17. Interior wood trim in a building is MOST often made of

    A. hemlock   B. pine   C. cedar   D. oak

18. Gaskets are seldom made of

    A. rubber   B. lead   C. asbestos   D. vinyl

19. Toggle bolts are MOST frequently used to

    A. fasten shelf supports to a hollow block wall
    B. fasten furniture legs to table tops
    C. anchor machinery to a concrete floor
    D. join two pieces of sheet metal

20. Rubber will deteriorate FASTEST when it is constantly in contact with

    A. air   B. water   C. oil   D. soapsuds

21. Stoppage of water flow is often caused by dirt <u>accumulating</u> in an elbow.
    As used in the above sentence, the word <u>accumulating</u> means MOST NEARLY

    A. clogging   B. collecting   C. rusting   D. confined

22. The surface of the metal was <u>embossed</u>.
    As used in the above sentence, the word <u>embossed</u> means MOST NEARLY

    A. polished   B. rough   C. raised   D. painted

Questions 23-24.

DIRECTIONS: Questions 23 and 24 are to be answered in accordance with the following paragraph.

When fixing an upper sash cord, you must also remove the lower sash. To do this, the parting strip between the sash must be removed. Now remove the cover from the weight box channel, cut off the cord as before, and pull it over the pulleys. Pull your new cord over the pulleys and down into the channel, where it may be fastened to the weight. The cord for an upper sash is cut off 1" or 2" below the pulley with the weight resting on the floor of the pocket and the cord held taut. These measurements allow for slight stretching of the cord. When the cord is cut to length, it can be pulled up over the pulley and tied with a single common knot in the end to fit into the socket in the sash groove. If the knot protrudes beyond the face of the sash, tap it gently to flatten. In this way, it will not become frayed from constant rubbing against the groove.

23. When repairing the upper sash cord, the FIRST thing to do is to

    A. remove the lower sash
    B. cut the existing sash cord
    C. remove the parting strip
    D. measure the length of new cord necessary

24. According to the above paragraph, the rope may become frayed if the

    A. pulley is too small   B. knot sticks out
    C. cord is too long   D. weight is too heavy

25. In the repair of the sash cord mentioned in the paragraph for Questions 23 and 24, the MAIN reason for cutting off the sash cord below the bottom of the pulley is to

    A. prevent the cord from tangling
    B. save on amount of cord used
    C. prevent the sash weight from hitting the bottom of the frame in use
    D. provide room for tying the knot

26. Of the following drawings, the one that would be considered an *elevation* of a building is the

    A. floor plan   B. front view   C. cross section   D. site plan

27. On a plan, the symbol shown at the right USUALLY represents a(n)

    A. duplex receptacle   B. electric switch
    C. ceiling outlet   D. pull box

28. On a plan, the symbol _____ - _____ - USUALLY represents a

   A. center line
   B. hidden outline
   C. long break
   D. dimension line

29. Assume that on a plan you see the following: 1/4" - 20 NC-2. This refers to the

   A. diameter of a hole
   B. size and type of screw thread
   C. taper of a pin
   D. scale at which the plan is drawn

30.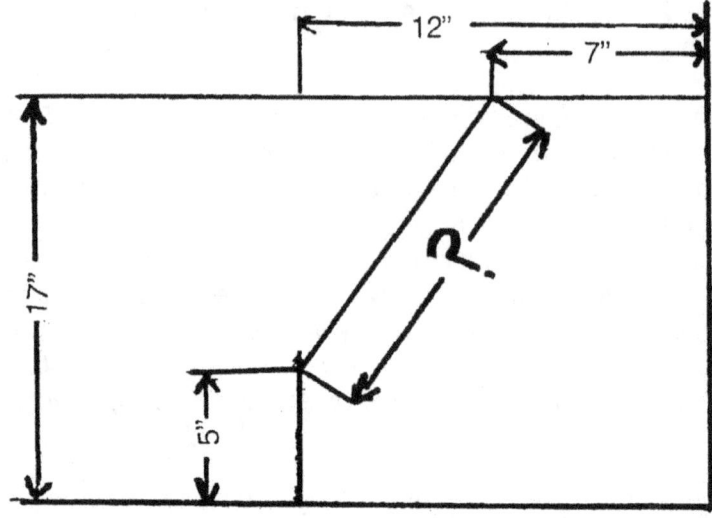

   In reference to the above sketch, the length of the diagonal part of the plate indicated by the question mark is MOST NEARLY

   A. 13"   B. 14"   C. 15"   D. 16"

31. To increase the workability of concrete without changing its strength, the BEST procedure to follow is to increase the percentage of

   A. water
   B. cement and sand
   C. cement and water
   D. water and sand

32. The MAIN reason for covering freshly poured concrete with tar paper is to

   A. prevent evaporation of water
   B. stop people from walking on the concrete
   C. protect the concrete from rain
   D. keep back any earth that may fall on the concrete

33. The MAIN reason for using air-entrained cement in sidewalks is to

   A. protect the concrete from the effects of freezing
   B. color the concrete
   C. speed up the setting time of the concrete
   D. make the concrete more workable

34. Assume that a reinforcing bar used for concrete is badly rusted. Before using this bar,

    A. it is not necessary to remove any rust
    B. only loose rust need be removed
    C. all rust should be removed
    D. all rust should be removed and a coat of red lead paint is applied

35. Assume that freshly poured concrete has been exposed to freezing temperatures for 6 hours.
    In all likelihood, this concrete

    A. has been permanently damaged
    B. will harden properly as soon as the air temperature warms up
    C. will harden properly even though the temperature remains below freezing
    D. will eventually harden properly, but it will take much longer than usual

36. Assume that concrete for a floor in a play yard is to be placed directly on the earth. On checking, you find that, because of a recent rain, the earth is damp.
    You should

    A. wait till the sun dries the earth before placing the concrete
    B. use a waterproofing material between the concrete slab and the earth
    C. use less water in the concrete mix
    D. ignore the damp earth and place the concrete as you normally would

37. The MAJOR disadvantage of *floating* the surface of concrete too much is that the

    A. surface will become too rough
    B. surface will become weak and will wear rapidly
    C. initial set will be disturbed
    D. concrete cannot be cured properly

38. In addition to water and sand, mortar mix for a cinder block wall is usually made of

    A. gravel and lime   B. plaster and cement
    C. gravel and cement   D. lime and cement

39. The *nominal* size of a standard cinder block is

    A. 8" x 6" x 16"   B. 8" x 8" x 16"
    C. 8" x 12" x 12"   D. 6" x 8" x 12"

40. The *bond* of a brick wall refers to the

    A. arrangement of headers and stretchers
    B. time it takes for the mortar to set
    C. way a brick wall is tied in to an intersecting wall
    D. type of mortar used in the wall

41. The purpose of *tooling* when erecting a brick wall is to

    A. cut the brick to fit into a small space
    B. insure that the brick is laid level
    C. compact the mortar at the joints
    D. hold the brick in place till the mortar sets

42. Mortar is BEST cleaned off the face of a brick wall by using

    A. muriatic acid   B. lye
    C. oxalic acid   D. sodium hypochlorite

43. A brick wall is *pointed* to

    A. make sure it is the correct height
    B. repair the mortar joints
    C. set the brick in place
    D. arrange the mortar bed before setting the brick

44. The second coat in a three-coat plaster job is the _____ coat.

    A. scratch   B. brown   C. putty   D. lime

45. To repair fine cracks in a plastered wall, the PROPER material to use is

    A. lime   B. cement wash
    C. perlite   D. spackle

46. Gypsum lath for plastering is purchased in

    A. strips 5/16" x 1 1/2" x 4'
    B. rolls 3/8" x 48" x 96"
    C. boards 1/2" x 16" x 48"
    D. sheets 5/16" x 27" x 96"

47. The PRINCIPAL reason for using acoustic tile instead of ordinary tile is that the acoustic tile

    A. deadens sound   B. is easier to apply
    C. is longer lasting   D. costs less

48. The MAXIMUM thickness of the finish coat of white plaster is MOST NEARLY

    A. 1/8"   B. 1/4"   C. 3/8"   D. 1/2"

49. When using tape to conceal joints in dry wall construction, the FIRST operation is

    A. channelling the grooves between boards
    B. applying cement to the joints
    C. sanding the edges of the joints
    D. packing the tape into the joints

50. For the FIRST coat of plaster on wire lath, plaster of paris is mixed with

    A. cement   B. sand   C. lime   D. mortar

KEY (CORRECT ANSWERS)

1. A	11. B	21. B	31. C	41. C
2. C	12. C	22. C	32. A	42. A
3. B	13. A	23. C	33. A	43. B
4. D	14. C	24. B	34. B	44. B
5. C	15. D	25. C	35. A	45. D
6. A	16. D	26. B	36. D	46. C
7. B	17. B	27. C	37. B	47. A
8. B	18. D	28. A	38. D	48. A
9. A	19. A	29. B	39. B	49. B
10. B	20. C	30. A	40. A	50. B

EXAMINATION SECTION
TEST 1

DIRECTIONS: Each question or incomplete statement is followed by several suggested answers or completions. Select the one that BEST answers the question or completes the statement. *PRINT THE LETTER OF THE CORRECT ANSWER IN THE SPACE AT THE RIGHT.*

Questions 1-5.

DIRECTIONS: For Questions 1 through 5, inclusive, Column I lists frequently used construction terms. Column II lists some of the building trades. For each item listed in Column I, enter in the appropriate space at the right the capital letter in front of the trade listed in Column II that is MOST closely associated with the item. Each trade may be used more than once or not at all.

COLUMN I	COLUMN II	
1. Bed	A. Plumbing	1.____
2. Wiping	B. Plastering	2.____
3. Brown	C. Carpentry	3.____
4. Key	D. Masonry	4.____
5. Bridging	E. Painting	5.____
	F. Steelwork	
	G. Roofing	

6. A *cricket* would be found   6.____

    A. on a roof
    B. at a structural steel connection
    C. supporting reinforcing steel
    D. over a window

7. *Cutting in* is done when   7.____

    A. trimming a stud to size
    B. fitting a bat in a brick wall
    C. painting in tight corners
    D. trimming tallow for a wiped joint

8. *Corbeling* results in   8.____

    A. strengthening a concrete column
    B. waterproofing a foundation wall
    C. anchoring a steel girder to a bearing wall
    D. increasing the thickness of a brick wall

9. Solder used for copper gutters is MOST frequently

   A. 30-70   B. 40-60   C. 50-50   D. 60-40

10. A jack rafter runs from

    A. plate to ridge   B. hip to ridge
    C. plate to hip   D. plate to plate

11. The one of the following items that is LEAST related to the others is

    A. sill   B. joist   C. sole   D. newel

12. A *fire cut* is made on

    A. timber posts   B. rafters
    C. floor joists   D. lathing

13. The one of the following items that is LEAST related to the others is

    A. joist hanger   B. pintle
    C. bridle iron   D. stirrup

14. The PROPER order of nailing sub-flooring and bridging is

    A. top of bridging, bottom of bridging, sub-flooring
    B. bottom of bridging, sub-flooring, top of bridging
    C. top of bridging, sub-flooring, bottom of bridging
    D. bottom of bridging, top of bridging, sub-flooring

15. Sleepers would be found in

    A. walls   B. doors   C. footings   D. floors

16. The one of the following woods that is MOST commonly used for finish flooring is

    A. hemlock   B. cypress   C. larch   D. oak

17. Spacing of studs in a stud partition is MOST frequently _____" o.c.

    A. 12   B. 14   C. 16   D. 18

18. A hollow masonry wall should be used in preference to a solid masonry wall when the characteristic MOST desired is

    A. insulation   B. strength
    C. beauty   D. durability

19. The arrangement of headers and stretchers in brickwork is known as the

    A. bond   B. stringer   C. lacing   D. stile

20. Of the following, the reason that is LEAST likely to justify pointing brickwork is that pointing _____ the wall.

    A. improves the appearance of
    B. helps prevent cracking of
    C. increases the useful life of
    D. helps waterproof

21. The purpose of flashing is to 21.____

    A. keep water out   B. speed the set of mortar
    C. anchor a cornice   D. cover exposed joists

22. The one of the following classes of wall that would LEAST likely be the outside wall of a building is a 22.____

    A. spandrel   B. fire   C. curtain   D. parapet

23. Lime is added to mortar USUALLY to 23.____

    A. increase the strength of the mortar
    B. make the mortar water resistant
    C. make it easier to apply the mortar
    D. improve the appearance of the mortar joint

24. Efflorescence on the face of a brick wall is BEST removed by scrubbing with a solution of 24.____

    A. muriatic acid   B. sodium silicate
    C. oxalic acid   D. calcium oxide

25. The one of the following that is NOT a defect in painting is 25.____

    A. chalking   B. checking
    C. alligatoring   D. waning

26. The one of the following ingredients of a paint that would be called the *vehicle* is 26.____

    A. white lead   B. turpentine
    C. linseed oil   D. pigment

27. The one of the following that is used as a rust preventative in the prime coat for painting steel is 27.____

    A. aluminum   B. red lead
    C. titanium dioxide   D. carbon black

28. *Boxing*, with reference to paint, means 28.____

    A. thinning   B. mixing   C. spreading   D. drying

29. When painting new wood, filling of nail holes and cracks with putty should be done 29.____

    A. 24 hours before priming
    B. immediately before priming
    C. after priming and before the second coat
    D. after the second coat and before the finish coat

30. The one of the following that is the size of a reinforcing rod MOST commonly used in reinforced concrete construction is 30.____

    A. 1 3/4" ϕ B. 18 gauge   C. #9   D. 2 ST3

31. Honeycombing in concrete is USUALLY caused by 31.____

    A. too plastic a mix   B. high fall of concrete
    C. mixing too long   D. inadequate vibration

32. A concrete mix is indicated as 1:2:3 1/2 mix. The number *2* refers to the proportion by volume of

    A. water   B. cement   C. gravel   D. sand

33. Specifications for concrete mixes frequently call for the use of dry sand. The reason for this is that the additional water in wet sand will

    A. make it more difficult to place the concrete
    B. decrease the strength of the concrete
    C. cause the sand and stone to segregate
    D. increase the cost of waterproofing

34. Curing of concrete serves PRIMARILY to

    A. prevent freezing of the concrete
    B. permit early removal of forms
    C. delay setting of the concrete
    D. prevent evaporation of moisture

35. The MAIN reason that forms for concrete work are oiled is to

    A. *permit* easy removal of forms
    B. *prevent* rust marks on the concrete
    C. *prevent* bleeding of water
    D. *permit* easier vibration of the concrete

36. The one of the following terms that is LEAST related to the others is

    A. 5-ply   B. mastic
    C. vapor barrier   D. flashing

37. Before quicklime can be used for plaster, it must be

    A. slaked   B. burned   C. floated   D. glazed

38. When a hard plaster is required, as in halls, the one of the following that would MOST likely be used is

    A. lime   B. Keene's cement
    C. stucco   D. marbling

39. To give plaster a hard finish, hydrated lime is mixed with

    A. white cement   B. linseed oil putty
    C. white lead   D. plaster of paris

40. The purpose of a ground in plaster work is to

    A. provide a key for the plaster
    B. help the plasterer make an even wall
    C. prevent the plasterer's scaffold from slipping
    D. hold the loose plaster before it is placed

41. When a lightweight plaster is required, the one of the following fine aggregates that is MOST likely to be used is

    A. cinders
    B. sand
    C. talc
    D. vermiculite

42. Of the following fireproofing materials, the one which would be MOST frequently used to fireproof steel columns in a fireproof building is

    A. sheet rock
    B. vermiculite plaster
    C. brick
    D. rock lath

43. The one of the following items that is LEAST related to the others is

    A. rock wool
    B. wall board
    C. sheet rock
    D. rock lath

44. The first layer of plaster placed in a 3-coat plaster job is called the _____ coat.

    A. brown   B. scratch   C. hard   D. white

45. The one of the following symbols that represents a steel section which is MOST similar in appearance to a W section is

    A. U   B. L   C. I   D. Z

46. A plate used to connect two steel angles in a roof truss is known as a(n)

    A. angle iron
    B. gusset plate
    C. bearing plate
    D. tie bar

47. Steel beams are COMMONLY anchored to brick walls by

    A. government anchors
    B. tie rods
    C. eye bars
    D. anchor bolts

48. Rivet holes are lined up with a

    A. set screw
    B. ginnywink
    C. drift pin
    D. trivet

49. A sewer that carries BOTH storm water and sewage is called a _____ sewer.

    A. sanitary   B. flush   C. combined   D. mixed

50. A fresh air inlet for a house drainage system would be connected to the system

    A. just ahead of the house trap
    B. at each horizontal branch line
    C. at the top of the stack through the roof
    D. at the trap of each water closet

KEY (CORRECT ANSWERS)

1. D	11. D	21. A	31. D	41. D
2. A	12. C	22. B	32. D	42. B
3. B	13. B	23. C	33. B	43. A
4. B	14. C	24. A	34. D	44. B
5. C	15. D	25. D	35. A	45. C
6. A	16. D	26. C	36. C	46. B
7. C	17. C	27. B	37. A	47. A
8. D	18. A	28. B	38. B	48. C
9. C	19. A	29. C	39. D	49. C
10. C	20. B	30. C	40. B	50. A

TEST 2

DIRECTIONS: Each question or incomplete statement is followed by several suggested answers or completions. Select the one that BEST answers the question or completes the statement. *PRINT THE LETTER OF THE CORRECT ANSWER IN THE SPACE AT THE RIGHT.*

Questions 1-5.

DIRECTIONS: Column I consists of a list of trades, and Column II lists tools used in those trades. In the space at the right, opposite the number of the trade in Column I, write the letter preceding the tool of the trade in Column II.

COLUMN I		COLUMN II	
1. Carpenter	A.	Mop	1.____
2. Plumber	B.	Hawk	2.____
3. Plasterer	C.	Miter box	3.____
4. Bricklayer	D.	Shave-hook	4.____
5. Roofer	E.	Jointing tool	5.____

Questions 6-7.

DIRECTIONS: Questions 6 and 7 refer to the mortar joints shown below.

6. The mortar joint MOST frequently used on common brickwork is   6.____
   A. 1   B. 2   C. 3   D. 4

7. The mortar joint which would NOT usually be made unless an outside scaffold was used is   7.____
   A. 1   B. 2   C. 3   D. 4

8. A rectangular yard is 50'0" long by 8'6" wide.   8.____
   The area of the yard is, in square feet,
   A. 420.0   B. 422.5   C. 425.0   D. 427.5

95

9. A rectangular court is 23'0" long by 9'6" wide. The length of the diagonal is MOST NEARLY

   A. 24'8"   B. 24'10"   C. 25'2"   D. 25'6"

10. Concrete weighs 150 pounds per cubic foot.
    A slab of concrete 6'0" long by 3'6" wide by 1'4" thick weighs MOST NEARLY _____ pounds.

    A. 4150   B. 4200   C. 4250   D. 4300

11. A building 32'0" by 65'0" occupies a lot 60'0" by 110'0". The ratio of building area to lot area is MOST NEARLY

    A. 0.32   B. 0.33   C. 0.34   D. 0.35

12. When painting wood, puttying of nail holes and cracks is done

    A. before any painting is started
    B. after the priming coat is applied
    C. after the finish coat is applied
    D. at any stage in the painting

13. The process of pouring paint from one container to another in order to mix it is known as

    A. bleeding   B. boxing   C. cutting   D. stirring

14. Paint is *thinned* with

    A. linseed oil   B. turpentine
    C. varnish   D. gasoline

15. A wood screw which can be tightened by a wrench is known as a _____ screw.

    A. lag   B. Philips   C. carriage   D. monkey

16. To permit easy removal of forms from concrete, the inside surfaces of the forms are often coated with

    A. paint   B. oil   C. water   D. asphalt

17. Sixteen pieces of 2 x 4 lumber, each 10'6" long, contain a total of _____ FBM.

    A. 110   B. 111   C. 112   D. 113

18. The consistency of concrete is measured with a

    A. Vicat needle   B. slump cone
    C. hook gage   D. bourdon gage

19. End-matched lumber would MOST likely be used for

    A. sheathing   B. roofing   C. flooring   D. siding

20. A post or shore is to be placed midway between columns to support the formwork for a reinforced concrete girder. The post should be cut

    A. short, so that wedging is required
    B. to exact length

C. long, so that it will have to be driven into place
D. in two pieces, to permit jackknifing into place

21. Batter boards are set by a

    A. mason   B. plumber   C. roofer   D. surveyor

22. Of the following terms, all of which refer to tools, the one which is LEAST related to the others is

    A. back   B. box-end   C. cross-cut   D. rip

23. Of the following tools, the one which is LEAST like the others is

    A. brace and bit
    B. draw-knife
    C. plans
    D. spoke-shave

24. When wood splits easily, it is advisable to drill a hole for each nail. The hole for the nail should be _____ the nail.

    A. larger in diameter than
    B. smaller in diameter than
    C. exactly the same diameter as
    D. less than one-quarter the length of

25. The length of a 10-penny nail, in inches, is

    A. $2\frac{1}{2}$ B. 3   C. $3\frac{1}{2}$ D. 4

26. The decimal equivalent of 31/64 of an inch is MOST NEARLY

    A. 0.45   B. 0.46   C. 0.47   D. 0.48

27. Of the following, the one which is BEST classified as an abrasive is

    A. a saw   B. a chisel   C. graphite   D. sandpaper

28. Of the following construction materials, the one which would MOST likely be stored directly on the ground is

    A. brick   B. cement   C. steel   D. wood

29. The strength of brick walls is based upon the type of mortar used. The relative strength of the various types of mortar, in descending order, is

    A. cement, lime, cement-lime
    B. lime, cement-lime, cement
    C. cement-lime, cement, lime
    D. cement, cement-lime, lime

30. Coating reinforcing rods with oil before placing them in the forms is

    A. *good* practice, because it prevents rusting
    B. *poor* practice, because it makes the rods difficult to handle
    C. *good* practice if the forms are oiled
    D. *poor* practice, because it destroys the bond between the concrete and the rods

31. If the mixing plant should break down after one-half the concrete has been mixed for a floor, the BEST thing to do would be to

   A. take the concrete out of the forms and throw it away
   B. spread the available concrete evenly over the floor area
   C. block off one-half of the floor area and place the available concrete in the blocked-off area
   D. keep mixing the concrete in the forms with shovels until the plant is repaired

32. Splicing of reinforcing bars is accomplished by

   A. using wire ties
   B. underlapping the bars
   C. hooking the bars
   D. using metal clips

33. A sanitary sewer carries

   A. storm water only
   B. sewage only
   C. sewage and storm water
   D. the discharge from a sewage plant

34. A neat line

   A. is the result of good workmanship
   B. is used in concrete construction only
   C. defines an outer limit of a structure
   D. defines an outer limit of excavation for a structure

35. Continued trowelling of a cement-finish floor for a building is

   A. *good* practice, because it provides a smooth floor
   B. *poor* practice, because it produces a slippery floor
   C. *poor* practice, because it brings the fines to the surface
   D. *good* practice, because it insures proper mixing of the cement finish

36. In reinforced concrete form work, a beveled chamfer strip is used to

   A. reinforce the outside of the forms
   B. reinforce the inside of the forms
   C. seal leaks in the forms
   D. do none of the foregoing

37. Cracks in lumber due to contraction along annual rings are known as

   A. checks
   B. wanes
   C. pitch pockets
   D. dry rot

38. Honeycombing is MOST likely to occur in construction involving

   A. steel   B. concrete   C. wood   D. masonry

39. Floor beams are sometimes crowned to

   A. provide arch action
   B. eliminate deflection
   C. strengthen the floor
   D. provide a more nearly level floor than would be provided by straight beams

40. In brickwork, a rowlock course consists of

    A. headers
    B. stretchers
    C. bricks laid on edge
    D. bricks laid so that the longest dimension is vertical

41. The term *bond,* as used in bricklaying, refers to

    A. structure only
    B. pattern only
    C. structure and pattern
    D. color and finish of individual bricks

42. Concrete is a mixture of cement,

    A. fine aggregate, coarse aggregate, and water
    B. sand, and water
    C. stone, and water
    D. sand, and stone

43. Consistency, when used in connection with concrete, refers to the

    A. seven-day strength
    B. twenty-eight day strength
    C. initial set before forms are removed
    D. plasticity of freshly mixed concrete

44. Brick may be used for the facing material in both faced walls and veneered walls. The distinction between the two types of walls relates to

    A. bonding or lack of bonding between facing and backing
    B. type of material in facing and backing
    C. relative thickness of facing and backing
    D. the type of mortar used

45. A plaster *key* is NOT formed on _____ lath.

    A. wood   B. metal
    C. expanded metal D. gypsum

46. Of the following, the BEST tool to use to make a hole in a coping stone is a

    A. star drill   B. coping saw
    C. pneumatic grinder D. diamond wheel dresser

47. Roughing refers to work performed by a

    A. carpenter B. bricklayer
    C. plumber   D. roofer

48. A post supporting a handrail is known as a

    A. tread   B. riser   C. newel   D. bevel

49. The live load on a floor is 40 pounds per square foot. The floor joists are on a 14'0" span and are spaced 2'6" on centers.
The maximum live load carried by a joist, in pounds, is MOST NEARLY

   A. 700   B. 933   C. 1167   D. 1400

50. Of the following terms, the one LEAST related to the others is

   A. ground
   B. purlin
   C. rafter
   D. ridge board

KEY (CORRECT ANSWERS)

1. C	11. A	21. D	31. C	41. C
2. D	12. B	22. B	32. A	42. A
3. B	13. B	23. A	33. B	43. D
4. E	14. B	24. B	34. C	44. A
5. A	15. A	25. B	35. C	45. D
6. C	16. B	26. D	36. D	46. A
7. A	17. C	27. D	37. A	47. C
8. C	18. B	28. A	38. B	48. C
9. B	19. C	29. D	39. D	49. D
10. B	20. A	30. D	40. C	50. A

READING COMPREHENSION
UNDERSTANDING AND INTERPRETING WRITTEN MATERIAL
EXAMINATION SECTION
TEST 1

DIRECTIONS: Each question or incomplete statement is followed by several suggested answers or completions. Select the one that BEST answers the question or completes the statement. *PRINT THE LETTER OF THE CORRECT ANSWER IN THE SPACE AT THE RIGHT.*

Questions 1-3.

DIRECTIONS: Questions 1 through 3, inclusive, are to be answered in accordance with the following paragraph.

All cement work contracts, more or less, in setting. The contraction in concrete walls and other structures causes fine cracks to develop at regular intervals. The tendency to contract increases in direct proportion to the quantity of cement in the concrete. A rich mixture will contract more than a lean mixture. A concrete wall which has been made of a very lean mixture and which has been built by filling only about one foot in depth of concrete in the form each day will frequently require close inspection to reveal the cracks.

1. According to the above paragraph,

    A. shrinkage seldom occurs in concrete
    B. shrinkage occurs only in certain types of concrete
    C. by placing concrete at regular intervals, shrinkage may be avoided
    D. it is impossible to prevent shrinkage

2. According to the above paragraph, the one of the factors which reduces shrinkage in concrete is the

    A. volume of concrete in wall
    B. height of each day's pour
    C. length of wall
    D. length and height of wall

3. According to the above paragraph, a rich mixture

    A. pours the easiest
    B. shows the largest amount of cracks
    C. is low in cement content
    D. need not be inspected since cracks are few

Questions 4-6.

DIRECTIONS: Questions 4 through 6, inclusive, are to be answered SOLELY on the basis of the following paragraph.

It is best to avoid surface water on freshly poured concrete in the first place. However, when there is a very small amount present, the recommended procedure is to allow it to evaporate before finishing. If there is considerable water, it is removed with a broom, belt, float, or by other convenient means. It is never good practice to sprinkle dry cement, or a mixture of cement and fine aggregate, on concrete to take up surface water. Such fine materials form a layer on the surface that is likely to dust or hair check when the concrete hardens.

4. The MAIN subject of the above passage is

   A. surface cracking of concrete
   B. evaporation of water from freshly poured concrete
   C. removing surface water from concrete
   D. final adjustments of ingredients in the concrete mix

5. According to the above passage, the sprinkling of dry cement on the surface of a concrete mix would MOST LIKELY

   A. prevent the mix from setting
   B. cause discoloration on the surface of the concrete
   C. cause the coarse aggregate to settle out too quickly
   D. cause powdering and small cracks on the surface of the concrete

6. According to the above passage, the thing to do when considerable surface water is present on the freshly poured concrete is to

   A. dump the concrete back into the mixer and drain the water
   B. allow the water to evaporate before finishing
   C. remove the water with a broom, belt, or float
   D. add more fine aggregate but not cement

Questions 7-9.

DIRECTIONS: Questions 7 through 9, inclusive, are to be answered ONLY in accordance with the information given in the paragraph below.

Before placing the concrete, check that the forms are rigid and well braced and place the concrete within 45 minutes after mixing it. Fill the forms to the top with the wearing-course concrete. Level off the surfaces with a strieboard. When the concrete becomes stiff but still workable (in a few hours), finish the surface with a wood float. This fills the hollows and compacts the concrete and produces a smooth but gritty finish. For a non-gritty and smoother surface (but one that is more slippery when wet), follow up with a steel trowel after the water sheen from the wood-troweling starts to disappear. If you wish, slant the tread forward a fraction of an inch so that it will shed rain water.

7. Slanting the tread a fraction of an inch gives a surface that will

   A. have added strength
   B. not be slippery when wet
   C. shed rain water
   D. not have hollows

8. In addition to giving a smooth but gritty finish, the use of a wood float will tend to   8._____

   A. give a finish that is slippery when wet
   B. compact the concrete
   C. give a better wearing course
   D. provide hollows to retain rain water

9. Which one of the following statements is most nearly correct?   9._____

   A. Having checked the forms, one may place the concrete immediately after mixing same.
   B. One must wait at least 15 minutes after mixing the concrete before it may be placed in the forms.
   C. A gritty compact finish and one which is more slippery when wet will result with the use of a wood float.
   D. A steel trowel used promptly after a wood float will tend to give a non-gritty smooth finish.

Questions 10-11.

DIRECTIONS: Questions 10 and 11 are to be answered SOLELY on the basis of information contained in the following paragraph.

Tools and plastering methods have changed very little over the years. Most of the changes are mere improvements of the basic tools. The tools formerly made by hand are now machine-made and are *rigidly* constructed of light, but strong, materials in contrast to the clumsy constructions of the early types. The power-driven mixers and hoisting equipment used on large plastering jobs today produce better mortars and lighten the tasks involved.

10. According to the above paragraph, present day tools used for plastering   10._____

    A. have made plastering much more complicated than it used to be
    B. are heavier than the old-fashioned tools they replaced
    C. produce poorer results but speed up the job
    D. are lighter and stronger than the hand-made tools of the past

11. As used in the above paragraph, the word *rigidly* means MOST NEARLY   11._____

    A. feeble   B. weakly   C. firmly   D. flexibly

Questions 12-18.

DIRECTIONS: Questions 12 through 18 are to be answered in accordance with the following paragraphs.

SURFACE RENEWING OVERLAYS

A surface renewing overlay should consist of material which can be constructed in very thin layers. The material must fill surface voids and provide an impervious skid-resistant surface. It must also be sufficiently resistant to traffic abrasion to provide an economical service life.

Materials meeting these requirements are:
    a. Asphalt concrete having small particle size
    b. Hot sand asphalts
    c. Surface seal coats

Fine-graded asphalt concrete or hot sand asphalt can be constructed in layers as thin as one-half inch and fulfill all requirements for surface renewing overlays. They are recommended for thin resurfacing of pavements having high traffic volumes, as their service lives are relatively long when constructed properly. They can be used for minor leveling, they are quiet riding, and their appearance is exceptionally pleasing. Seal coats or slurry seals may fulfill surface requirements for low traffic pavements.

12. A surface renewing overlay must fill surface voids, provide an impervious skid-resistant surface, and

    A. be resistant to traffic abrasion
    B. have small particle size
    C. be exceptionally pleasing in appearance
    D. be constructed in half-inch layers

13. An *impervious skid-resistant surface* means a surface that is

    A. rough to the touch and fixed firmly in place
    B. waterproof and provides good gripping for tires
    C. not damaged by skidding vehicles
    D. smooth to the touch and quiet riding

14. The number of types of materials that can be constructed in very thin layers and are also suitable for surface renewing overlays is

    A. 1   B. 2   C. 3   D. 4

15. The SMALLEST thickness of asphalt concrete or hot sand asphalt that can fulfill all requirements for surface renewing overlays is _____ inch(es).

    A. ¼   B. ½   C. 1   D. 2

16. The materials that are recommended for thin resurfacing of pavements having high traffic volumes are

    A. those that have relatively long service lives
    B. asphalt concretes with maximum particle size
    C. surface seal coats
    D. slurry seals with voids

17. Fine-graded asphalt concrete and hot sand asphalt are quiet riding and are also

    A. recommended for low traffic pavements
    B. used as slurry seal coats
    C. suitable for major leveling
    D. exceptionally pleasing in appearance

18. The materials that may fulfill surface requirements for low traffic pavements are 18._____

    A. fine-graded asphalt concretes
    B. hot sand asphalts
    C. seal coats or slurry seals
    D. those that can be used for minor leveling

Questions 19-25.

DIRECTIONS: Questions 19 through 25 are to be answered SOLELY on the basis of the paragraphs below.

OPEN-END WRENCHES

Solid, non-adjustable wrenches with openings in one or both ends are called open-end wrenches. Wrenches with small openings are usually shorter than wrenches with large openings. This proportions the lever advantage of the wrench to the bolt or stud and helps prevent wrench breakage or damage to the bolt or stud.

Open-end wrenches may have their jaws parallel to the handle or at angles anywhere up to 90 degrees. The average angle is 15 degrees. This angular displacement variation permits selection of a wrench suited for places where there is room to make only a part of a complete turn of a nut or bolt. Handles are usually straight, but may be curved. Those with curved handles are called S-wrenches. Other open-end wrenches may have offset handles. This allows the head to reach nut or bolt heads that are sunk below the surface.

There are a few basic rules that you should keep in mind when using wrenches. They are:
    I. ALWAYS use a wrench that fits the nut properly. Otherwise, the wrench may slip, or the nut may be damaged.
    II. Keep wrenches clean and free from oil. Otherwise, they may slip, resulting in possible serious injury to you or damage to the work.
    III. Do NOT increase the leverage of a wrench by placing a pipe over the handle. Increased leverage may damage the wrench or the work.

19. Open-end wrenches 19._____

    A. are adjustable
    B. are solid
    C. always have openings at both ends
    D. are always S-shaped

20. Wrench proportions are such that wrenches with _____ openings have _____ handles. 20._____

    A. larger; shorter   B. smaller; longer
    C. larger; longer   D. smaller; thicker

21. The average angle between the jaws and the handle of a wrench is _____ degrees. 21._____

    A. 0   B. 15   C. 22   D. 90

22. Offset handles are intended for use MAINLY with

   A. offset nuts
   B. bolts having fine threads
   C. nuts sunk below the surface
   D. bolts that permit limited swing

23. The wrench which is selected should fit the nut properly because this

   A. prevents distorting the wrench
   B. insures use of all wrench sizes
   C. avoids damaging the nut
   D. overstresses the bolt

24. Oil on wrenches is

   A. *good* because it prevents rust
   B. *good* because it permits easier turning
   C. *bad* because the wrench may slip off the nut
   D. *bad* because the oil may spoil the work

25. Extending the handle of a wrench by slipping a piece of pipe over it is considered

   A. *good* because it insures a tight nut
   B. *good* because less effort is needed to loosen a nut
   C. *bad* because the wrench may be damaged
   D. *bad* because the amount of tightening can not be controlled

KEY (CORRECT ANSWERS)

1.	D	11.	C
2.	B	12.	A
3.	B	13.	B
4.	C	14.	C
5.	D	15.	B
6.	C	16.	A
7.	C	17.	D
8.	B	18.	C
9.	A	19.	B
10.	D	20.	C

21. B
22. C
23. C
24. C
25. C

TEST 2

DIRECTIONS: Each question or incomplete statement is followed by several suggested answers or completions. Select the one that BEST answers the question or completes the statement. *PRINT THE LETTER OF THE CORRECT ANSWER IN THE SPACE AT THE RIGHT.*

Questions 1-3.

DIRECTIONS: Questions 1 through 3 are to be answered SOLELY on the basis of the following passage.

    A utility plan is a floor plan which shows the layout of a heating, electrical, plumbing, or other utility system. Utility plans are used primarily by the persons reponsible for the utilities, but they are important to the craftsman as well. Most utility installations require the leaving of openings in walls, floors, and roofs for the admission or installation of utility features. The craftsman who is, for example, pouring a concrete foundation wall must study the utility plans to determine the number, sizes, and locations of the openings he must leave for piping, electric lines, and the like.

1. The one of the following items of information which is LEAST likely to be provided by a utility plan is the

    A. location of the joists and frame members around stairwells
    B. location of the hot water supply and return piping
    C. location of light fixtures
    D. number of openings in the floor for radiators

2. According to the passage, the persons who will *most likely* have the GREATEST need for the information included in a utility plan of a building are those who

    A. maintain and repair the heating system
    B. clean the premises
    C. paint housing exteriors
    D. advertise property for sale

3. According to the passage, a repair crew member should find it MOST helpful to consult a utility plan when information is needed about the

    A. thickness of all doors in the structure
    B. number of electrical outlets located throughout the structure
    C. dimensions of each window in the structure
    D. length of a roof rafter

Questions 4-9.

DIRECTIONS: Questions 4 through 9 are to be answered SOLELY on the basis of the following passage.

    The basic hand-operated hoisting device is the tackle or purchase, consisting of a line called a fall, reeved through one or more blocks. To hoist a load of given size, you must set up a rig with a safe working load equal to or in excess of the load to be hoisted. In order to do this, you must be able to calculate the safe working load of a single part of line of given size, the safe working load of a given purchase which contains a line of given size, and the minimum size of hooks or shackles which you must use in a given type of purchase to hoist a given load. You must also be able to calculate the thrust which a given load will exert on a gin pole or a set of shears inclined at a given angle, the safe working load which a spar of a given size used as a gin pole or as one of a set of shears will sustain, and the stress which a given load will set up in the back guy of a gin pole or in the back guy of a set of shears inclined at a given angle.

4. The above passage refers to the lifting of loads by means of

    A. erected scaffolds   B. manual rigging devices
    C. power-driven equipment   D. conveyor belts

5. It can be concluded from the above passage that a set of shears serves to

    A. absorb the force and stress of the working load
    B. operate the tackle
    C. contain the working load
    D. compute the safe working load

6. According to the above passage, a spar can be used for a

    A. back guy   B. block   C. fall   D. gin pole

7. According to the above passage, the rule that a user of hand-operated tackle MUST follow is to make sure that the safe working load is AT LEAST

    A. equal to the weight of the given load
    B. twice the combined weight of the block and falls
    C. one-half the weight of the given load
    D. twice the weight of the given load

8. According to the above passage, the two parts that make up a tackle are

    A. back guys and gin poles   B. blocks and falls
    C. rigs and shears   D. spars and shackles

9. According to the above passage, in order to determine whether it is safe to hoist a particular load, you MUST

    A. use the maximum size hooks
    B. time the speed to bring a given load to a desired place
    C. calculate the forces exerted on various types of rigs
    D. repeatedly lift and lower various loads

Questions 10-15.

DIRECTIONS: Questions 10 through 15 are to be answered SOLELY on the basis of the following set of instructions.

PATCHING SIMPLE CRACKS IN A BUILT-UP ROOF

If there is a visible crack in built-up roofing, the repair is simple and straightforward:

1. With a brush, clean all loose gravel and dust out of the crack, and clean three or four inches around all sides of it.
2. With a trowel or putty knife, fill the crack with asphalt cement and then spread a layer of asphalt cement about 1/8 inch thick over the cleaned area.
3. Place a strip of roofing felt big enough to cover the crack into the wet cement and press it down firmly.
4. Spread a second layer of cement over the strip of felt and well past its edges.
5. Brush gravel back over the patch.

10. According to the above passage, in order to patch simple cracks in a built-up roof, it is necessary to use a

    A. putty knife and a drill
    B. knife and pliers
    C. tack hammer and a punch
    D. brush and a trowel

11. According to the above passage, the size of the area that should be clear of loose gravel and dust before the asphalt cement is first applied should

    A. be the exact size of the crack itself
    B. extend three or four inches on all sides of the crack
    C. be 1/8 inch greater than the size of the crack itself
    D. extend the length of the roofing strip

12. According to the above passage, loose gravel and dust in the crack should be removed with a

    A. brush
    B. felt pad
    C. trowel
    D. dust mop

13. Assume that both layers of asphalt cement needed to patch the crack are of the same thickness.
    The total thickness of asphalt cement used in the patch should be MOST NEARLY _____ inch.

    A. 1/2
    B. 1/3
    C. 1/4
    D. 1/8

14. According to the instructions in the above passage, how large should the strip of roofing felt be cut?

    A. Three of four inches square
    B. Smaller than the crack and small enough to be surrounded by cement on all sides of the strip
    C. Exactly the same size and shape of the area covered by the wet cement
    D. Large enough to completely cover the crack

15. The final or finishing action to be taken in patching a simple crack in a built-up roof is to

    A. clean out the inside of the crack
    B. spread a layer of asphalt a second time
    C. cover the crack with roofing felt
    D. cover the patch of roofing felt and cement with gravel

Questions 16-17.

DIRECTIONS: Questions 16 and 17 are to be answered SOLELY on the basis of the information given in the following paragraph.

Supplies are to be ordered from the stockroom once a week. The standard requisition form, Form SP21, is to be used for ordering all supplies. The form is prepared in triplicate, one white original and two green copies. The white and one green copy are sent to the stockroom, and the remaining green copy is to be kept by the orderer until the supplies are received.

16. According to the above paragraph, there is a limit on the

    A. amount of supplies that may be ordered
    B. day on which supplies may be ordered
    C. different kinds of supplies that may be ordered
    D. number of times supplies may be ordered in one year

17. According to the above paragraph, when the standard requisition form for supplies is prepared,

    A. a total of four requisition blanks is used
    B. a white form is the original
    C. each copy is printed in two colors
    D. one copy is kept by the stock clerk

Questions 18-21.

DIRECTION: Questions 18 through 21 are to be answered SOLELY on the basis of the following passage.

The Oil Pollution Act for U. S. waters defines an *oily mixture* as 100 parts or more of oil in one million parts of mixture. This mixture is not allowed to be discharged into the prohibited zone. The prohibited zone may, in special cases, be extended 100 miles out to sea but, in general, remains at 50 miles offshore. The United States Coast Guard must be contacted to report all *oily mixture* spills. The Federal Water Pollution Control Act provides for a fine of $10,000 for failure to notify the United States Coast Guard. An employer may take action against an employee if the employee causes an *oily mixture* spill. The law holds your employer responsible for either cleaning up or paying for the removal of the oil spillage.

18. According to the Oil Pollution Act, an *oily mixture* is defined as one in which there are _____ parts or more of oil in _____ parts of mixture.

    A. 50; 10,000
    B. 100; 10,000
    C. 100; 1,000,000
    D. 10,000; 1,000,000

19. Failure to notify the proper authorities of an *oily mixture* spill is punishable by a fine. Such fine is provided for by the

    A. United States Coast Guard
    B. Federal Water Pollution Control Act
    C. Oil Pollution Act
    D. United States Department of Environmental Protection

20. According to the law, the one responsible for the removal of an *oily mixture* spilled into U.S. waters is the

    A. employer
    B. employee
    C. U.S. Coast Guard
    D. U.S. Pollution Control Board

21. The *prohibited zone,* in general, is the body of water

    A. within 50 miles offshore
    B. beyond 100 miles offshore
    C. within 10,000 yards of the coastline
    D. beyond 10,000 yards from the coastline

Questions 22-25.

DIRECTIONS: Questions 22 through 25 are to be answered SOLELY on the basis of the following paragraph.

Synthetic detergents are materials produced from petroleum products or from animal or vegetable oils and fats. One of their advantages is the fact that they can be made to meet a particular cleaning problem by altering the foaming, wetting, and emulsifying properties of a cleaner. They are added to commonly used cleaning materials such as solvents, water, and alkalies to improve their cleaning performance. The adequate wetting of the surface to be cleaned is paramount in good cleaning performance. Because of the relatively high surface tension of water, it has poor wetting ability, unless its surface tension is decreased by addition of a detergent or soap. This allows water to flow into crevices and around small particles of soil, thus loosening them.

22. According to the above paragraph, synthetic detergents are made from all of the following EXCEPT

    A. petroleum products   B. vegetable oils
    C. surface tension oils   D. animal fats

23. According to the above paragraph, water's poor wetting ability is related to

    A. its low surface tension
    B. its high surface tension
    C. its vegetable oil content
    D. the amount of dirt on the surface to be cleaned

24. According to the above paragraph, synthetic detergents are added to all of the following EXCEPT

    A. alkalines   B. water   C. acids   D. solvents

25. According to the above paragraph, altering a property of a cleaner can give an advantage in meeting a certain cleaning problem.
The one of the following that is NOT a property altered by synthetic detergents is the cleaner's

    A. flow ability
    B. foaming property
    C. emulsifying property
    D. wetting ability

25.____

KEY (CORRECT ANSWERS)

1. A
2. A
3. B
4. B
5. A

6. D
7. A
8. B
9. C
10. D

11. B
12. A
13. C
14. D
15. D

16. D
17. B
18. C
19. B
20. A

21. A
22. C
23. B
24. C
25. A

ARITHMETICAL REASONING

EXAMINATION SECTION
TEST 1

DIRECTIONS: Each question or incomplete statement is followed by several suggested answers or completions. Select the one that BEST answers the question or completes the statement. *PRINT THE LETTER OF THE CORRECT ANSWER IN THE SPACE AT THE RIGHT.*

1. If it takes 2 men 9 days to do a job, how many men are needed to do the same job in 3 days?

    A. 4   B. 5   C. 6   D. 7

    1._____

2. Suppose that a department operates 1,644 buildings. If one employee is needed for every 2 buildings, and one foreman is needed for every 18 employees, the number of foremen needed is CLOSEST to

    A. 45   B. 50   C. 55   D. 60

    2._____

3. If 60 bars of soap cost the same as 2 gallons of wax, how many bars of soap can be bought for the price of 5 gallons of wax?

    A. 120   B. 150   C. 180   D. 300

    3._____

4. An employee waxes 275 sq.ft. of floor on Monday, 352 sq.ft. on Tuesday, 179 sq.ft. on Wednesday, and 302 sq.ft. on Thursday.
   In order to average 280 sq.ft. of floor waxed a day, how many square feet of floor must he wax on Friday?

    A. 264   B. 278   C. 292   D. 358

    4._____

5. A project covers 35 acres altogether. Lawns, playgrounds, and walks take up 28 acres and the rest is given over to buildings.
   What percentage of the total area is given over to buildings?

    A. 7%   B. 20%   C. 25%   D. 28%

    5._____

6. When preparing for a mopping operation, fill the standard 16 quart bucket to the 3/4 full mark with warm water. Then add detergent at the rate of 2 oz. per gallon of water and disinfectant at the rate of 1 oz. to 3 gallons of water. According to these directions, the amount of detergent and disinfectant to add to 3/4 of a bucket of warm water is _____ oz. detergent and _____ oz. disinfectant.

    A. 4; 1/2   B. 5; 3/4   C. 6; 1   D. 8; 1 1/4

    6._____

7. If corn brooms weigh 32 lbs. a dozen, the average weight of one corn broom is CLOSEST to _____ lbs. _____ oz.

    A. 2; 14   B. 2; 11   C. 2; 9   D. 2; 6

    7._____

8. At the beginning of the year, a foreman has 7 dozen electric bulbs in stock. During the year, he receives a shipment of 14 dozen bulbs, and also replaces 5 burned out bulbs a month in each of 3 buildings in his area. How many electric bulbs does he have on hand at the end of the year? _____ dozen. 8._____

   A. 3   B. 6   C. 8   D. 12

9. A project has 4 buildings, each 14 floors high. Each floor has 10 apartments. If 35% of the apartments in the project have 3 rooms or less, how many apartments have 4 or more rooms? 9._____

   A. 196   B. 210   C. 364   D. 406

10. An employee takes 1 hour and 30 minutes a day to sweep 30 flights of stairs. How many flights of stairs does he sweep in a month if he spends a total of 30 hours doing this job and works at the same rate? 10._____

    A. 200   B. 300   C. 600   D. 900

11. During a month, Employee A washed 30 windows, Employee B washed 4 times as many windows as Employee A, and Employee C washed half as many windows as Employee B. The TOTAL number of windows washed by all three men together during this month is 11._____

    A. 180   B. 210   C. 240   D. 330

12. How much would it cost to completely fence in the playground area shown at the right with fencing costing $7.50 a foot? 12._____

    A. $615.00
    B. $820.00
    C. $885.00
    D. $960.00

    (Figure: L-shaped playground with dimensions 14 ft, 9 ft, 26 ft, 33 ft)

13. A drill bit measures .625 inches. The fractional equivalent, in inches, is 13._____

    A. 9/16   B. 5/8   C. 11/16   D. 3/4

14. The number of cubic yards of sand required to fill a bin measuring 12 feet by 6 feet by 4 feet is MOST NEARLY 14._____

    A. 8   B. 11   C. 48   D. 96

15. Assume that you are assigned to put down floor tiles in a room measuring 8 feet by 10 feet. Individual tiles measure 9 inches by 9 inches. The total number of floor tiles required to cover the entire floor is MOST NEARLY 15._____

    A. 107   B. 121   C. 142   D. 160

16. Lumber is usually sold by the board foot, and a board foot is defined as a board one foot square and one inch thick.
    If the price of one board foot of lumber is 90 cents and you need 20 feet of lumber 6 inches wide and 1 inch thick, the cost of the 20 feet of lumber is

    A. $9.00   B. $12.00   C. $18.00   D. $24.00

17. For a certain plumbing repair job, you need three lengths of pipe, 12 1/4 inches, 6 1/2 inches, and 8 5/8 inches.
    If you cut these three lengths from the same piece of pipe, which is 36 inches long, and each cut consumes 1/8 inch of pipe, the length of pipe REMAINING after you have cut out your three pieces should be _____ inches.

    A. 7 1/4   B. 7 7/8   C. 8 1/4   D. 8 7/8

18. A maintenance bond for a roadway pavement is in an amount of 10% of the estimated cost.
    If the estimated cost is $8,000,000, the maintenance bond is

    A. $8,000   B. $80,000   C. $800,000   D. $8,000,000

19. Specifications require that a core be taken every 700 square yards of paved roadway or fraction thereof. A 100 foot by 200 foot rectangular area would require _____ core(s).

    A. 1   B. 2   C. 3   D. 4

20. An applicant must file a map at a scale of 1" = 40'. Six inches on the map represents _____ feet on the ground.

    A. 600   B. 240   C. 120   D. 60

21. A 100' x 110' lot has an area of MOST NEARLY _____ acre.

    A. 1/8   B. 1/4   C. 3/8   D. 1/2

22. 1 inch is MOST NEARLY equal to _____ feet.

    A. .02   B. .04   C. .06   D. .08

23. The area of the triangle EFG shown at the right is MOST NEARLY _____ sq. ft.

    A. 36   B. 42   C. 48   D. 54

24. Specifications state: As further security for the faithful performance of this contract, the Comptroller shall deduct, and retain until the final payment, 10% of the value of the work certified for payment in each partial payment voucher, until the amount so deducted and retained shall equal 5% of the contract price or in the case of a unit price contract, 5% of the estimated amount to be paid to the Contractor under the contract.
    For a $300,000 contract, the amount to be retained at the end of the contract is

    A. $5,000   B. $10,000   C. $15,000   D. $20,000

25. Asphalt was laid for a length of 210 feet on the entire width of a street whose curb-to-curb distance is 30 feet. The number of square yards covered with asphalt is MOST NEARLY

    A. 210   B. 700   C. 2,100   D. 6,300

KEY (CORRECT ANSWERS)

1. C
2. A
3. B
4. C
5. B

6. C
7. B
8. B
9. C
10. C

11. B
12. C
13. B
14. B
15. C

16. A
17. C
18. C
19. D
20. B

21. B
22. D
23. A
24. C
25. B

SOLUTIONS TO PROBLEMS

1. $(2)(9) = 18$ man-days. Then, $18 \div 3 = 6$ men

2. The number of employees = $1644 \div 2 = 822$. The number of foremen needed = $822 \div 18 \approx 45$

3. 1 gallon of wax costs the same as $60 \div 2 = 30$ bars of soap. Thus, 5 gallons of wax costs the same as $(5)(30) = 150$ bars of soap.

4. To average 280 sq.ft. for five days means a total of $(5)(280) = 1400$ sq.ft. for all five days. The number of square feet to be waxed on Friday = $1400 - (275+352+179+302) = 292$

5. The acreage for buildings is $35 - 28 = 7$. Then, $7/35 = 20\%$

6. $(16)(3/4) = 12$ quarts = 3 gallons. The amount of detergent, in ounces, is $(2)(3) = 6$. The amount of disinfectant is 1 oz.

7. One corn broom weighs $32 \div 12 = 2\ 2/3$ lbs. $\approx$ 2 lbs. 11 oz.

8. Number of bulbs at the beginning of the year = $(7)(12) + (14)(12) = 252$. Number of bulbs replaced over an entire year = $(5)(3)(12) = 180$. The number of unused bulbs = $252 - 180 = 72 = 6$ dozen.

9. Total number of apartments = $(4)(14)(10) = 560$. The number of apartments with at least 4 rooms = $(.65)(560) = 364$.

10. $30 \div 1\ 1/2 = 20$. Then, $(20)(30) = 600$ flights of stairs

11. The number of windows washed by A, B, C were 30, 120, and 60. Their total is 210.

12. The two missing dimensions are $26 - 14 = 12$ ft. and $33 - 9 = 24$ ft. Perimeter = $9 + 12 + 33 + 26 + 24 + 14 = 118$ ft. Thus, total cost of fencing = $(118)(\$7.50) = \$885.00$

13. $.625 = \dfrac{625}{1000} = \dfrac{5}{8}$

14. $(12)(6)(4) = 288$ cu.ft. Now, 1 cu.yd. = 27 cu.ft.; 288 cu.ft. is equivalent to $10\ 2/3$ or about 11 cu.yds.

15. 144 sq.in. = 1 sq.ft. The room measures (8 ft.)x(10 ft.) = 80 sq.ft. = 11,520 sq.in. Each tile measures $(9)(9) = 81$ sq.in. The number of tiles needed = $11,520 \div 81 = 142.2$ or about 142.

16. 20 ft. by 6 in. = (20 ft.)(1/2 ft.) = 10 sq.ft. Then, $(10 \times .90) = \$9.00$

17. There will be 3 cuts in making 3 lengths of pipe, and these 3 cuts will use $(3)(1/8) = 3/8$ in. of pipe. The amount of pipe remaining after the 3 pieces are removed = $36 - 12\ 1/4 - 6\ 1/2 - 8\ 5/8 - 3/8 = 8\ 1/4$ in.

18. The maintenance bond = $(.10)(\$8,000,000) = \$800,000$

19. $(100)(200) = 20,000$ sq.ft. $= 20,000 \div 9 \approx 2222$ sq.yds. Then, $2222 \div 700 \approx 3.17$. Since a core must be taken for each 700 sq.yds. plus any left over fraction, 4 cores will be needed.

20. Six inches means $(6)(40) = 240$ ft. of actual length.

21. $(100 \text{ ft.})(110 \text{ ft.}) = 11,000$ sq.ft. ≈ 1222 sq.yds. Then, since 1 acre = 4840 sq.yds., 1222 sq.yds. is equivalent to about 1/4 acre.

22. 1 in. = 1/12 ft. $\approx$ .08 ft.

23. Area of $\triangle$ EFG = $(1/2)(8)(6) + (1/2)(4)(6) = 36$ sq.ft.

24. The amount to be retained = $(.05)(\$300,000) = \$15,000$

25. $(210)(30) = 6300$ sq.ft. Since 1 sq.yd. = 9 sq.ft., 6300 sq.ft. equals 700 sq.yds.

TEST 2

DIRECTIONS: Each question or incomplete statement is followed by several suggested answers or completions. Select the one that BEST answers the question or completes the statement. *PRINT THE LETTER OF THE CORRECT ANSWER IN THE SPACE AT THE RIGHT.*

1. The TOTAL length of four pieces of 2" pipe, whose lengths are 7'3 1/2", 4'2 3/16", 5'7 5/16", and 8'5 7/8", respectively, is

    A. 24'6 3/4"
    B. 24'7 15/16"
    C. 25'5 13/16"
    D. 25'6 7/8"

    1._____

2. Under the same conditions, the group of pipes that gives the SAME flow as one 6" pipe is (neglecting friction) _____ pipes.

    A. 3 3" B. 4 3" C. 2 4" D. 3 4"

    2._____

3. A water storage tank measures 5' long, 4' wide, and 6' deep and is filled to the 5 1/2' mark with water.
If one cubic foot of water weighs 62 pounds, the number of pounds of water required to COMPLETELY fill the tank is

    A. 7,440 B. 6,200 C. 1,240 D. 620

    3._____

4. A hot water line made of copper has a straight horizontal run of 150 feet and, when installed, is at a temperature of 45°F. In use, its temperature rises to 190°F.
If the coefficient of expansion for copper is 0.0000095" per foot per degree F, the total expansion, in inches, in the run of pipe is given by the product of 150 multiplied by 0.0000095 by

    A. 145
    B. 145 x 12
    C. 145 divided by 12
    D. 145 x 12 x 12

    4._____

5. To dig a trench 3'0" wide, 50'0" long, and 5'6" deep, the total number of cubic yards of earth to be removed is MOST NEARLY

    A. 30 B. 90 C. 140 D. 825

    5._____

6. If it costs $65 for 20 feet of subway rail, the cost of 150 feet of this rail will be

    A. $487.50 B. $512.00 C. $589.50 D. $650.00

    6._____

7. The number of cubic feet of concrete it takes to fill a form 10 feet long, 3 feet wide, and 6 inches deep is

    A. 12 B. 15 C. 20 D. 180

    7._____

8. The sum of 4 1/16, 5 1/4, 3 5/8, and 4 7/16 is

    A. 17 3/16 B. 17 1/4 C. 17 5/16 D. 17 3/8

    8._____

9. If you earn $10.20 per hour and time and one-half for working over 40 hours, your gross salary for a week in which you worked 42 hours would be

    A. $408.00 B. $428.40 C. $438.60 D. $770.80

    9._____

10. A drill bit, used to drill holes in track ties, has a diameter of 0.75 inches. When expressed as a fraction, the diameter of this drill bit is

   A. 1/4"   B. 3/8"   C. 1/2"   D. 3/4"

11. Three dozen shovels were purchased for use.
    If the shovels were used at the rate of nine a week, the number of weeks that the three dozen lasted was

   A. 3   B. 4   C. 9   D. 12

12. Assume that you earn $20,000 per year.
    If twenty percent of your pay is deducted for taxes, social security, and pension, your weekly take-home pay will be MOST NEARLY

   A. $280   B. $308   C. $328   D. $344

13. If a measurement scaled from a drawing is one inch, and the scale of the drawing is 1/8 inch to the foot, then the one inch measurement would represent an ACTUAL length of

   A. 8 feet   B. 2 feet
   C. 1/8 of a foot   D. 8 inches

14. Tiles 12" x 12" are used to lay a floor having the dimensions 10'0" x 12'0". The MINIMUM number of tiles needed to completely cover the floor is

   A. 60   B. 96   C. 120   D. 144

15. The volume of concrete in a strip of sidewalk 30 feet long by 4 feet wide by 3 inches thick is _____ cubic feet.

   A. 30   B. 120   C. 240   D. 360

16. To change a quantity of cubic feet into an equivalent quantity of cubic yards, _____ the quantity by _____.

   A. multiply; 9   B. divide; 9
   C. multiply; 27   D. divide; 27

17. If a pump can deliver 50 gallons of water per minute, then the time needed for this pump to empty an excavation containing 5,800 gallons of water is _____ hour(s) _____ minutes.

   A. 2; 12   B. 1; 56   C. 1; 44   D. 1; 32

18. The sum of 3 1/6", 4 1/4", 3 5/8", and 5 7/16" is

   A. 15 9/16"   B. 16 1/8"   C. 16 23/48"   D. 16 3/4"

19. If a measurement scaled from a drawing is 2 inches, and the scale of the drawing is 1/8 inch to the foot, then the two inch measurement would represent an ACTUAL length of

   A. 8 feet   B. 4 feet
   C. 1/4 of a foot   D. 16 feet

20. A room is 7'6" wide by 9'0" long with a ceiling height of 8'0". One gallon of flat paint will cover approximately 400 square feet of wall.
    The number of gallons of this paint required to paint the walls of this room, making no deductions for windows or doors, is MOST NEARLY

    A. 1/4 B. 1/2 C. 2/3 D. 1

21. The cost of a certain job is broken down as follows:

    Materials $3,750
    Rental of equipment 1,200
    Labor   3,150

    The percentage of the total cost of the job that can be charged to materials is MOST NEARLY

    A. 40% B. 42% C. 44% D. 46%

22. By trial, it is found that by using two cubic feet of sand, a 5 cubic foot batch of concrete is produced. Using the same proportions, the amount of sand required to produce 2 cubic yards of concrete is MOST NEARLY _____ cubic feet.

    A. 20 B. 22 C. 24 D. 26

23. It takes 4 men 6 days to do a certain job.
    Working at the same speed, the number of days it will take 3 men to do this job is

    A. 7 B. 8 C. 9 D. 10

24. The cost of rawl plugs is $27.50 per gross. The cost of 2,448 rawl plugs is

    A. $467.50 B. $472.50 C. $477.50 D. $482.50

25. In a certain district, the area of a building may be no longer than 55% of the area of the lot on which it stands. On a rectangular lot 75 ft. by 125 ft., the maximum permissible area of building is, in square feet, MOST NEARLY

    A. 5,148 B. 5,152 C. 5,156 D. 5,160

KEY (CORRECT ANSWERS)

1.	D	11.	B
2.	B	12.	B
3.	D	13.	A
4.	A	14.	C
5.	A	15.	A
6.	A	16.	D
7.	B	17.	B
8.	D	18.	C
9.	C	19.	D
10.	D	20.	C

21. D
22. B
23. B
24. A
25. C

SOLUTIONS TO PROBLEMS

1. $3\frac{1}{6}" + 4\frac{1}{4}" + 3\frac{5}{8}" + 5\frac{7}{16}" + = 3\frac{8}{48}" + 4\frac{12}{48}" + 3\frac{30}{48}" + 5\frac{21}{48}" = 15\frac{71}{48}" = 16\frac{23}{48}"$

2. The flow of a 6" pipe is measured by the cross-sectional area. Since diameter = 6", radius = 3", and so area = 9 π sq.in. A single 3" pipe would have a cross-sectional area of (3/2) π sq.in. = 2.25 π sq.in. Now, 9 ÷ / 2.25 = 4. Thus, four 3" pipes is equivalent, in flow, to one 6" pipe.

3. (5x4x6) - (5x4x5 1/2) = 10. Then, (10)(62) = 620 pounds.

4. The total expansion = (150')(.0000095"/1 ft.)(190°-45°). So, the last factor is 145.

5. (3')(50')(5 1/2') = 825 cu.ft. Since 1 cu.yd. = 27 cu.ft., 825 cu.ft. cu.yds.

6. 150 ÷ 20 = 7.5. Then, (7.5)($65) = $487.50

7. (10')(3')(1/2') = 15 cu.ft.

8. $4\frac{1}{16} + 5\frac{4}{16} + 3\frac{10}{16} + 4\frac{7}{16} = 16\frac{22}{16} = 17\frac{3}{8}$

9. Gross salary = ($10.20)(40) + ($15.30)(2) = $438.60

10. $75" = \frac{75}{100}" = \frac{3}{4}"$

11. 3 dozen = 36 shovels. Then, 36 ÷ 9 = 4 weeks

12. Since 20% is deducted, the take-home pay = ($20,000)(.80) = $16,000 for the year, which is $16,000 ÷ 52 ≈ $308 per week.

13. A scale drawing where 1/8" means an actual size of 1 ft. implies that a scale drawing of 1" means an actual size of (1')(8) = 8'

14. (10')(12') = 120 sq.ft. Since each tile is 1 sq.ft., a total of 120 tiles will be used.

15. (30')(4')(1/4') = 30 cu.ft.

16. To convert a given number of cubic feet into an equivalent number of cubic yards, divide by 27.

17. 5800 ÷ 50 = 116 min. = 1 hour 56 minutes

18. $3\frac{1}{6}" + 4\frac{1}{4}" + 3\frac{5}{8}" + 5\frac{7}{16}" + = 3\frac{8}{48}" + 4\frac{12}{48}" + 3\frac{30}{48}" + 5\frac{21}{48}" = 15\frac{71}{48}" = 16\frac{23}{48}"$

19. 2 ÷ 1/8 = 16, so a 2" drawing represents an actual length of 16 feet.

20. The area of the 4 walls = 2(7 1/2')(8') + 2(9')(8') = 264 sq.ft. Then, 264 ÷ 400 = .66 or about 2/3 gallon of paint.

21. $3750 + $1200 + $3150 = $8100. Then, $3750/$8100 ≈ 46%

22. 2 cu.yds. ÷ 5 cu.ft. = 54 ÷ 5 = 10.8. Now, (10.8)(2 cu.ft.) ≈ 22 cu.ft. Note: 2 cu.yds. = 54 cu.ft.

23. (4)(6) = 24 man-days. Then, 24 ÷ 3 = 8 days

24. 2448 ÷ 144 = 17. Then, (17)($27.50) = $467.50

25. (75')(125') = 9375 sq.ft. The maximum area of the building = (.55)(9375 sq.ft.) * 5156 sq.ft.

TEST 3

DIRECTIONS: Each question or incomplete statement is followed by several suggested answers or completions. Select the one that BEST answers the question or completes the statement. *PRINT THE LETTER OF THE CORRECT ANSWER IN THE SPACE AT THE RIGHT.*

1. A steak weighed 2 pounds, 4 ounces. How much did it cost at $4.60 per pound?
   A. $7.80   B. $8.75   C. $9.90   D. $10.35

2. twenty pints of water just fill a pail. the capacity of the pail, in gallons, is
   A. 2   B. 2 1/4   C. 2 1/2   D. 2 3/4

3. The sum of 5/12 and 1/4 is
   A. 7/12   B. 2/3   C. 3/4   D. 5/6

4. The volume of earth, in cubic yards, excavated from a trench 4'0" wide by 5'6" deep by 18'6" long is MOST NEARLY
   A. 14.7   B. 15.1   C. 15.5   D. 15.9

5. 5/8 written as a decimal is
   A. 62.5   B. 6.25   C. .625   D. .0625

6. The number of cubic feet in a cubic yard is
   A. 9   B. 12   C. 27   D. 36

7. If it costs $16.20 to lay one square yard of asphalt, to lay a patch 15' by 15', it will cost MOST NEARLY
   A. $405.00   B. $3,645.00   C. $134.50   D. $243.00

8. You are assigned thirty (30) asphalt workers to be divided into two crews so that one crew will have 2/3 as many men as the other. The number of men you would put into the SMALLER crew is
   A. 10   B. 12   C. 14   D. 20

9. It takes 12 asphalt workers, working 6 hours a day, 5 days to complete a certain job. The number of days it will take 10 men, working 8 hours a day, to do the same job, assuming all work at the same rate, is
   A. 2 1/2   B. 3   C. 4 1/2   D. 6

10. A street is laid to a 3% grade. This means that in 150 ft., the street grade will rise
    A. 4 1/2 inches   B. 45 inches
    C. 4 1/2 feet   D. 45 feet

11. The sum of the following dimensions, 3 4/8, 4 1/8, 5 1/8, and 6 1/4, is

    A. 19   B. 19 1/8   C. 19 1/4   D. 19 1/2

12. A worker is paid $9.30 per hour.
    If he works 8 hours each day on Monday, Tuesday, and Wednesday, 3 1/2 hours on Thursday, and 3 hours on Friday, the TOTAL amount due him is

    A. $283.65   B. $289.15   C. $276.20   D. $285.35

13. The price of metal lath is $395.00 per 100 square yards. The cost of 527 square yards of this lath is MOST NEARLY

    A. $2,076.50   B. $2,079.10   C. $2,081.70   D. $2,084.30

14. The total cost of applying 221 square yards of plaster board is $3,430.
    The cost per square yard is MOST NEARLY

    A. $14.00   B. $14.50   C. $15.00   D. $15.50

15. In a three-coat plaster job, the scratch coat is 1/8 in. thick in front of the lath, the brown coat is 3/16 in. thick, and the finish coat is 1/8 in. thick.
    The TOTAL thickness of this plaster job, measured from the face of the lath, is

    A. 7/16"   B. 1/2"   C. 9/16"   D. 5/8"

16. If an asphalt worker earns $38,070 per year, his wages per month are MOST NEARLY

    A. $380.70   B. $735.00   C. $3,170.00   D. $3,807.00

17. The sum of 4 1/2 inches, 3 1/4 inches, and 7 1/2 inches is 1 foot _____ inches.

    A. 3   B. 3 1/4   C. 3 1/2   D. 4

18. The area of a rectangular asphalt patch, 9 ft. 3 in. by 6 ft. 9 in., is _____ square feet.

    A. 54   B. 54 1/4   C. 54 1/2   D. 62 7/16

19. The number of cubic feet in a cubic yard is

    A. 3   B. 9   C. 16   D. 27

20. A 450 ft. long street with a grade of 2% will have one end of the street higher than the other end by _____ feet.

    A. 2   B. 44   C. 9   D. 20

21. If the drive wheel of a roller is 6 ft. in diameter and the tiller wheel is 4 ft. in diameter, whenever the drive wheel makes a complete revolution on a straight pass, the tiller wheel makes _____ revolution(s).

    A. 1   B. 1 1/4   C. 1 1/2   D. 2

22. A point on the centerline of a street is marked: Station 42 + 51. Another point on the centerline 30 feet from the first is marked Station 42+81.
    A third should be marked Station

    A. 12+51   B. 42+21   C. 45+51   D. 72+51

23. In twenty minutes, a truck moving with a speed of 30 miles an hour will cover a distance of _____ miles. 23._____

    A. 3   B. 5   C. 10   D. 30

24. The number of pounds in a ton is 24._____

    A. 500   B. 1,000   C. 2,000   D. 5,000

25. During his summer vacation, a boy earned $45.00 per day and saved 60% of his earnings. 25._____
    If he worked 45 days, how much did he save during his vacation?

    A. $15.00   B. $18.00   C. $1,215.00   D. $22.50

KEY (CORRECT ANSWERS)

1. D   11. A
2. C   12. A
3. B   13. C
4. B   14. D
5. C   15. A

6. C   16. C
7. A   17. B
8. B   18. D
9. C   19. D
10. C   20. C

21. C
22. B
23. C
24. C
25. C

SOLUTIONS TO PROBLEMS

1. ($4.60)(2 1/4 lbs.) = $10.35

2. 1 gallon = 8 pints, so 20 pints = 20/8 = 2 1/2 gallons

3. $\dfrac{5}{12} + \dfrac{1}{4} = \dfrac{5}{12} + \dfrac{3}{12} = \dfrac{8}{12} = \dfrac{2}{3}$

4. (4')(5 1/2')(18 1/2') = 407 cu.ft. Since 1 cu.yd. = 27 cu.ft., 407 cu.ft. ≈ 15.1 cu.yds.

5. 5/8 = 5 ÷ 8.000 = .625

6. There are (3)(3)(3) = 27 cu.ft. in a cu.yd.

7. (15')(15') = 225 sq.ft. = 25 sq.yds. Then, ($16.20)(25) = $405.00

8. Let 2x = size of smaller crew and 3x = size of larger crew. Then, 2x + 3x = 30. Solving, x = 6. Thus, the smaller crew consists of 12 workers.

9. (12)(6)(5) = 360 worker-days. Then, 360 ÷ [(10)(8)] = 4 1/2 days

10. (.03)(150') = 4 1/2 ft.

11. $3\dfrac{4}{8} + 4\dfrac{1}{8} + 5\dfrac{1}{8} + 6\dfrac{2}{8} = 18\dfrac{8}{8} = 19$

12. ($9.30)(8+8+8+3 1/2+3) = ($9.30)(30 1/2) = $283.65

13. The cost of 527 sq.yds. = (5.27)($395.00) = $2081.65 ≈ $2081.70

14. $3430 ÷ 221 ≈ $15.50

15. $\dfrac{1}{8}" + \dfrac{3}{16}" + \dfrac{1}{8}" = \dfrac{2}{16}" + \dfrac{3}{16}" + \dfrac{2}{16}" = \dfrac{7}{16}"$

16. $38,070 ÷ 12 = $3172.50 ≈ $3170.00 per month

17. 4 1/2" + 3 1/4" + 7 1/2" = 15 1/4" = 1 ft. 3 1/4 in.

18. 9 ft. 3 in. = 9 1/4 ft., 6 ft. 9 in. = 6 3/4 ft. Area = (9 1/4)(6 3/4) = 62 7/16 sq.ft.

19. A cubic yard = (3)(3)(3) = 27 cubic feet

20. (450')(.02) = 9 ft.

21. 6/4 = 1 1/2 revolutions

22. Station 42 + 51
    30 ft away would be 51 + 30 = 81 OR 51 - 30 = 21
    Station 42 + 81 or 42 + 21 (ANSWER: B)

23. 30 miles in 60 minutes means 10 miles in 20 minutes.

24. There are 2000 pounds in a ton.

25. ($45.00)(.60) = $27.00 savings per day. For 45 days, his savings is (45)($27.00) = $1215.00

www.ingramcontent.com/pod-product-compliance
Lightning Source LLC
Chambersburg PA
CBHW082208300426
44117CB00016B/2715